The Discovery of the Netherlands *for hil*

Henk

11-21-09

Henk van Os in collaboration with Huigen Leeflang and Jenny Reynaerts

The Discovery of the Netherlands

Four Centuries of Landscape Painting by Dutch masters

NAi Publishers Rotterdam

Contents

Foreword

Apeldoorn will be embraced by the first Apeldoorn International Triennial in the summer of 2008 which lasts for a hundred days. Culture, gardens and landscape will draw visitors from home and abroad to this 'town set in a green landscape', that likes to think of itself as the county town of the Netherlands' Veluwe, in the province of Gelderland. Apeldoorn is indeed bordered by expansive and varied landscape, and has a green heart adorned by many fine, tranquil parks.

We are delighted that the CODA Museum is presenting this exceptional exhibition 'The Discovery of the Netherlands' during the Triennial. For the exhibition Professor Henk van Os has made his own special selection of paintings from museums the world over. They are superb paintings in which, above all else, 'praises are sung' to the beauty of the Netherlands' landscape. With great care and consideration he drew up a list of priorities in collaboration with two curators from Amsterdam's Rijksmuseum who are experts in the field, dr Jenny Reynaerts and drs Huigen Leeflang.

Understandably, the most excellent and most interesting paintings are very important works; they are bound to belong to the museum's permanent exhibition and educational audio tour. So it was no easy task to persuade the museums to loan them for this show. It meant that, aside from his expertise, Henk van Os has had to use his powers of persuasion and his charm to ensure that these magnificent works might travel to Apeldoorn. The two curators also had to draw on their networks to ensure acquiring the finest and best works. I would like to extend my warmest thanks to the museums loaning the paintings. Without them this dream could not have been realized. For as far as we know this is the first time that around forty landscape paintings, covering four centuries of painterly tradition, have been brought together – and that makes this exhibition exceptionally interesting. It is also special in another way in that we were able to loan a number of works from private collections that we can now show to the public. I am extremely grateful to the owners for their generous contribution to our project. Who would have thought at the start of this project that we would be able to bring so many top works together in this exhibition?

In this book Henk van Os, in his own unsurpassed way, relates the story of four centuries of landscape painting. In her article his colleague, Louise Fresco from the University of Amsterdam, examines the notion that 'man

is the measure of all things' with regard to the specific paintings brought together in this exhibition. It has led to a fascinating dialogue.
The landscape of the Netherlands has also inspired many writers and poets. Included in this publication are appropriate and original quotations from Dutch poetry pertaining to the landscape. These quotations are not directly related to the paintings, but provide a form of literary enhancement and atmospheric description.

The first ideas for an event of this nature including garden and landscapes were born in 2002 during meetings to discuss the new cultural vision proposed by Apeldoorn Municipal Council.
All the participants at these gatherings reacted enthusiastically to the garden and landscape theme – one that seems to fit the town like a glove. The Triennial adds lustre and substance to Apeldoorn, adding another important aspect to this city's identity.

We at the CODA Museum are extremely pleased that so many knowledgeable and capable people have participated in this major project.
In addition to Henk van Os and his advisory panel, I would like to thank Wim Crouwel, who has supervised the graphic design both for the exhibition and the publication. I would also like to thank NAi Publishers for their production of a beautiful book to commemorate this project.

For such major projects we also rely on outside financial support. I would like to thank the Apeldoorn Triennial Foundation, the Prince Bernhard Cultural Fund, the VSB Fund and the Rabobank Apeldoorn for their generous contributions.
This exhibition invites you to rediscover the landscape of the Netherlands. I wish you great pleasure on this intriguing and delightful journey, this voyage of discovery covering four centuries of Dutch landscape painting.

Carin E.M. Reinders
Director of CODA

The Discovery of the Netherlands (1614–1944)

Henk van Os in collaboration with Huigen Leeflang and Jenny Reynaerts

The exhibition entitled 'The Discovery of the Netherlands' and this accompanying catalogue consider some of the paintings that contributed to the 'aesthetic reclamation' of the Netherlands. By means of their paintings and drawings, artists have opened up for us the intrinsic beauty of the Dutch landscape. Quite possibly there are artists who paint only what we, their viewers, find attractive. But it is equally true that artists are pioneers, exploring on our behalf and discovering the beauties of the landscape. They have reclaimed this largely flat countryside of the Netherlands, with its rivers, cities and marshy fields, its patches of woodland and huge skies with their ever-changing cloud formations – and they have transformed this into art.

Aesthetic Reclamation

The best-known example of aesthetic reclamation by artists is the discovery of the Alps. For Erasmus, travelling in the early sixteenth century through these mountains, they were nothing but an irritating hindrance between him and northern Italy. He journeyed southwards through the mountain passes, sitting in his carriage, and on the way back from Italy to England composed his famous work, *In Praise of Folly*, paying not the slightest heed to the imposing mountain peaks through which he passed. One of the first artists, however, who *was* inspired by the Alpine landscape, was Pieter Bruegel, who travelled in 1552 from Antwerp to Italy. Bruegel's biographer, the artist Karel van Mander, recounts how the former busied himself sketching and thus absorbing the landscape: he says it was as if Bruegel had swallowed all those mountains and cliffs only to spew them out again upon his canvases and panels once he returned home. In Bruegel's paintings and drawings we see fertile valleys enclosed by rocky cliffs but we do not see the really high mountains. Not until the second half of the eighteenth century do we find artists and poets awed by the mighty mountains when, leaving the built environment, they go in search of *the sublime*. At such moments people experience with a shiver their own insignificance, contrasted with the all-encompassing power of Nature. Taking their inspiration from writers and artists, scholarly ramblers explored new paths. Clubs were formed of eager walkers and mountain climbers, and, groups marched off cheerfully into the countryside; today the tradition continues with coachloads full of holiday tourists scrambling to the top of famous peaks.

There is a delightful story dating from the early seventeenth century describing the artist as mediator in people's appreciation of natural beauty. In a publication from 1628 about *Miniatura or the Art of Limning* the Englishman Edward Norgate tells a story about a citizen of Antwerp who went to see a friend who was a painter. This painter received 'The gentleman of Antwerpe' in his studio, and the latter, who had just returned from a trip into the Ardennes, began enthusiastically to describe his time in this beautiful mountainous district of Belgium. The painter, meanwhile, had started on a new picture. '[He] begins to paint, what the other spake . . .'. When the traveller had completed his story, it seems that something like the following took place: the artist lifted his canvas from the easel, turned it to face his friend and asked, 'Is this where you were?' The other was 'astonisht with wonder' and apparently replied, 'Yes, that's exactly what it looked like. How did you know? Have you been there too?' The artist answered, 'No, but you can only think the Ardennes are beautiful if they are painted in the way we generally portray mountain landscapes.' That is why, suggests Norgate, the discovery of landscape art is a useful and profitable 'noveltie'.

Norgate wished to make it clear through this story that the reason why we find a landscape beautiful is because artists have already 'discovered' this landscape, made a picture of it and framed nature for us. In doing this they have adapted the landscape according to their artistic principles. It is thanks to the way these artists have shaped their presentations of nature that we experience the beauty of the landscape.

From the Artists' Viewpoint

I should like to suggest three examples of the way in which landscape painting has affected our appreciation and experience of nature. One of the artists who made a major contribution to how we now react to the beauty of the landscape is the seventeenth-century Dutch painter Meindert Hobbema. He made detailed pictures of the landscape, using a coulisse construction, so that the viewers forget they are looking at a two-dimensional canvas and are led, as it were, into the space beyond the frame. Hobbema's paintings have greatly influenced the appreciation of this type of landscape, both among artists and art lovers. One such was Egbert van Drielst, who in the early nineteenth century applied the schemes of the great master when working in the province of Drente, in the northeast Netherlands. In his paintings he transformed this barren and poverty-stricken landscape into scenes of wondrous beauty. Not surprisingly, Van Drielst is known as the 'Drentse Hobbema'. Meindert Hobbema and Jacob van Ruisdael were the great heroes of the nineteenth-century English landscape artist, John Constable. Inspired by these two seventeenth-century Dutch painters, Constable took part of the English country of Suffolk and made it into the most famous landscape in England. Indeed, the area around Flatford and Dedham has gained the title: Constable Country. Recently in nearby Stoke-by-Nayland some trees were felled because their presence detracted from the view that Constable would have had when he painted there in 1837. The British newspaper *The Daily Telegraph* carried the headline: 'Trees to make way for view that inspired Constable'. Interestingly, John Constable opposed the setting up of London's National Gallery in 1824, for he argued that then it is the painters themselves who become the criterion and not nature. That is exactly what has happened with his work. He is the prime example of a painter who has shaped the British experience of nature. In the Netherlands, some guardians of our areas of outstanding natural beauty have a tendency to create a mise en scène of the countryside that has been entrusted to their care. Possibly they decide to preserve the site as it was at an ecologically interesting moment in its development, thus transforming nature into an historic landscape.

My third example is a personal one, and requires a little introduction. In the 1920s the province of Groningen had an authentic avant-garde artistic movement of its own. To simplify matters, these painters are generally all grouped together under the name of their association, *De Ploeg* (The Plough) and labelled 'expressionists'. The group wanted to express their rejection of the attitudes of the older generation of painters from the Groningen region; one way of doing this was geographical: rather than cycling southwards in search of landscapes to paint, they moved northwards. After all, the province of Drente had long been aesthetically reclaimed land – it was already a painter's landscape.

The artists of *De Ploeg* sought the unending spaces of the great north, the *Hoge Land*. In those days the northern stretches were solely used as agricultural land and no artist had ever considered painting them. But now they trekked out into the teeth of the wind and began creating their pictures of the flatlands of Reitdiepdal – to the astonishment of the local farmers. 'What art paintin', lad?' a farmer once asked Job Hansen, who was sitting outside in the farmer's fields, absorbed in making a picture. 'I am painting space', came the reply.

One of this group, Jan Altink, could well be named the Constable of the Netherlands' North. More than anyone else, he succeeded in suggesting both deep melancholy and soaring ecstasy with his wonderful paintings of the light that shimmers across this landscape. It was chiefly through his work that, as a schoolboy, I discovered how beautiful that part of the world is. And when in the early 1960s I wanted to live there, I found that few Groningers had been converted to the beauties of North Groningen province by the painters of *De Ploeg*. Everyone thought I was crazy. 'Why on earth go there?' was the most often-heard reaction. Not until ten years later did people – thanks to the *De Ploeg* painters – begin to discover this part of the country, the Reitdiep, including Hamming's café in Garnwerd. Recently, the Groninger Museum mounted an exhibition showing how the *De Ploeg* painters had revealed the northern landscape of Groningen province; visitors could rent a bicycle and ride out to look at the places they had just seen in the paintings. Then everyone realized: landscape painters aren't in the business of painting what people think is beautiful – no, they paint, and thanks to their work we discover what is beautiful.

The Discovery of the Netherlands Illustrated

No country was to take its own scenery and make it a subject for painting from such an early period, nor continue to paint it so systematically, as the Netherlands.

The discovery of the Alps was made by artists from elsewhere. These painters revealed the immense majesty of the Alpine ranges to romantically-minded travellers. But in the Netherlands as early as the beginning of the seventeenth century Dutch artists began to make pictorial records of their native land for the inhabitants of their country; thus they transformed their own small region into a beauteous realm. In the following centuries the whole of the Netherlands was gradually transferred onto canvas. Using around forty masterworks we plan to show the exceptional richness of Netherlandish landscape art and its significance in how people here experience the beauty of their country. We have therefore chosen paintings in which, whenever possible, a specific place could be identified. We aimed for high quality but also for as great as possible a diversity of scenes in order that we might show the breadth and range of Netherlandish landscape art.

It was not difficult to find the painting with which to start our landscape journey: the surroundings of the city which Samuel van Hoogstraeten in his book on painting *Hooge schoole der schilderkonst* (1678) so justly describes as 'Haarlem, birthplace of landscape artists'. From early times the surroundings of this city have been considered the cleanest, the healthiest and most beautiful Dutch countryside. After the city of Haarlem had thrown off the long-endured yoke of the Spanish Habsburgs, its reputation was enhanced. Both city and surrounding countryside had become safe, had become Dutch domain. In the dunes behind the coastline people could now disport themselves at ease, enjoying the natural beauty either on foot or in a carriage, passing well-known *'Plaisante Plaetsen'*, as described on the title page of one of the earliest series of prints showing Dutch landscapes in the Haarlem district. One of the very earliest pictorial representations of a pleasant outing in the dunes near Haarlem is a painting dating from 1614 by one of the forefathers of Northern Netherlandish landscape art, Esaias van de Velde. This work is, *p. 41* as it were, the starting post for a journey into the Netherlands landscape. The Haarlem region reappears in this exhibition in the picture showing the view over the lake of Haarlemmer Meer, where today the international airport of Schiphol covers the drained land. This painting was made by Jan van Goyen in 1646. It is one of the jewels of Dutch Golden Age *p. 45* painting, and now hangs in New York's Metropolitan Museum. Painted in almost monochrome hues with a fine brushstroke, the painting provides a magnificent impression of the wide flat polder landscape as it once was. The picture is built up from contrasting dark and light zones, producing a remarkable effect. Without fuss, without frills, it tells the viewer about the clouds, the sky, the land and the water of the Low Countries.

The image of a city that in large measure owed its fame and beauty to its location became a fixed formula for cityscapes of Haarlem and its surroundings, the finest examples being the so-called *Haerlempjes* painted by Ruisdael from around 1675. However, as early as 1646 Van Goyen shows us a city nestling within the countryside beneath a sky filled with impressive cloud formations, a city which dwarfs the shapes of windmills, farms, towers and Haarlem's Great Church outlined against it. The high viewpoint of the painting, the sense of immense space and especially the exceptionally convincing rendering of clouds and shafts of sunlight, all contribute to this relatively small painting's unprecedented statement about the Netherlandish landscape.

So that was the opening statement; it was more difficult to determine a conclusion for 'The Discovery of the Netherlands'. After all, there are many artists today engaged in painting the landscape of this country. But post-World War II, art carries a different cultural significance from before. Today we also have photography, and there is land art, and there are conceptual site-specific projects, and there is a great deal of non-figurative painting that is inspired by the landscape. At the very

least this gives a new context to landscape painting of specific scenes.
A possible end date could be the year 1900; by then the theory of Art for
Art's Sake had become generally accepted, thanks to the impressionists.
When the subject matter is no longer relevant and the painting becomes
a question of the way in which it is painted, of *how* rather than *what* –
why should you bother any more about the specific scene that is shown?
As far as Netherlandish artists are concerned, our great painters of
the late nineteenth and early twentieth century often made use of the
visual language of modern art of their time in order to present their
own experience of the landscape. This is true of such artists as those of
The Hague School as well as, for instance, Jan Toorop, Floris Verster and
Piet Mondrian.

Jan Weissenbruch, in an almost off-the-cuff pictorial observation of sails
near a small bridge at Nieuwkoop, has presented a typical Netherlandish *p. 109*
experience of light, space and colour. Jan Toorop made use of the stipple
technique adopted from neo-impressionism – a method developed in
order to analyse the effect of light in paintings – in order to render the
light in his painting of the view from the coastal harbour of Veere. *p. 111*
Piet Mondrian, in his early work, reproduced in an impressive manner
the structure of the Netherlandish landscape. 'Art for Art's Sake' or
not, the work of such artists has made an essential contribution to the
discovery of the Netherlands through art – and we honour them as great
landscape painters.

When we planned the exhibition we decided to conclude with the picture
showing the inundation of the countryside around Rotterdam in 1944, *p. 119*
painted by Hendrik Chabot. Not only is this a picture of a landscape that
is easily recognizable, it is also a landscape at an identifiable time, by one
of our greatest expressionist painters. Between these two moments – the
idyllic recreation scene in Haarlem's dunes from 1614 and the dramatic
scene near Rotterdam from the war year of 1944 – lies our 'discovery of
the Netherlands'.

People and Nature

In 2006 I mounted an exhibition for The Hague's Mauritshuis, entitled
'Dreaming of Italy', which presented around forty works spanning three
centuries by painters who left the chilly north and travelled southwards to
Italy in search of inspiration for their work. That exhibition taught me that
work by so-called Italianates only gains a genuine historical context when
you don't make it too easy for yourself by restricting your choices to only

one art-historically defined period but select with a long-term perspective. When planning the exhibition 'The Discovery of the Netherlands' we also chose for the *longue durée*. On the whole, exhibitions on the Netherlands landscape focus on one period or one theme. This time we offer the opportunity to compare masterworks from four centuries. Furthermore, in making our selection we decided to accentuate striking contrasts in the landscapes of different centuries.

An important difference between earlier centuries and today is that in seventeenth-century paintings town and country are presented as a unity. There is no question of unspoilt nature on the one hand and the intrusive human presence on the other, which we find in post-Romantic work. In Dutch Golden Age paintings we see a city's silhouette rising above an arcadian scene. A most moving example of this is the view of the town of Zwolle painted in 1675 by the little-known Hendrick ten Oever. *p. 63* The sun is setting, the countryside surrounding the town is presented as if it were Arcadia, with peaceful cows and happy people bathing naked in the waterways that intersect the fields. In an exceptional arrangement, the Talbot Rice Gallery of the University of Edinburgh has lent this painting for the exhibition.

One of the most impressive panoramic views of town and country ever painted in the Netherlands is the picture by Matthias Withoos of the city of Amersfoort in 1671. The obvious position for the painter to station *p. 61* himself when making such an overview of the city would have been on the raised ground of 'Mount Amersfoort' – the *Amersfoortse Berg*. But Withoos chose a lower viewpoint on the other side of the city because from there you had the best view of his town's trade and industry, of the boats on the lake, of the new buildings going up all around both for dwellings and for industrial mills, and the new bleaching fields – all of which brought prosperity to Amersfoort. Such sights filled the city fathers with satisfaction, as they gazed at the painting. What today we might easily call 'urban sprawl' was in the seventeenth century a cause for pride in your city. The extensive city fortifications were also presented as an object of urban pride.

A city that in the past was harassed by sieges contrives to construct strong defence works, but when in 1860 Johan Conrad Greive paints a *p. 89* defence work, he uses the bomb-proof barracks in Flushing as painterly architecture, as background to the beach where boats are being rigged. But 'rigging' suggest far greater human activity than the quietness of the painting permits. Human activity is hushed and is, as it were, absorbed into the expansive view out across the water. The picture is about serenity, hustle and bustle is banished far away. In this picture people are not characters with a part, as in seventeenth-century paintings; they convey a mood. The painting is above all a composition in browns and blues. One of the first landscape paintings of the northern Netherlands is by a burgomaster of the Frisian capital of Leeuwarden, Jacob Sibrandi Mancadan, and dates from 1650. In this case it seems highly probable *p. 53* that peat cutting activities inspired the depiction of this area in Friesland, now known as *Friese Wouden*. Mancadan was evidently less concerned about the poverty-stricken peat cutters than the economic results of their labour.

In 1649 Joris van der Haagen painted two pendant pictures, panoramic views of the Rhine landscape near the city of Arnhem. In these two works *p. 47, 49* the landscape is no longer regarded as an extension of the city but has a significance of its own. The paintings are astonishing in view of the date they were made in their powerful presentation of a specific landscape. It is striking how little Van der Haagen seems to have schematized his paintings. In the left-hand painting the trees at the left act as a repoussoir – something that leads the eye into a picture – for the viewer, whose gaze then continues into the background where the river Rhine meanders through the countryside. In the right-hand picture the house at the right acts as a concluding statement and the visual journey is ended. But these repoussoirs are not – as is so often the case – mere pieces of décor by means of which the painter creates the illusion of distance while in fact we are looking at a flat surface. They form an intrinsic part of the panorama. The visual journey through the land of Arnhem starts with a defence-work on the city walls, newly constructed in 1649. Joris van der Haagen must have climbed up the *Hoge Wal* beside the defence works in order to sketch his pictures of the Rhineland panorama. In the two paintings there are still many landscape features easily identifiable. Journeying through his landscapes you occasionally encounter someone – a carriage passes by, a solitary shepherd sits watching his flock, you meet a huntsman. These figures form an organic part of the landscape. I stress this point now because in later landscape painting it is often decidedly different.

In order to gain more understanding of the relation between people and landscape in seventeenth- and nineteenth-century paintings it is useful to compare two beach scenes, which are among the most beautiful ever painted in our country. In the beach scene by Adriaen van de Velde

we encounter people who are actively doing something – even if it's *p. 57*
only looking out to sea. The French historian Alain Corbin in his famous
study, *Le territoire du vide*, 1990 – in English *The Lure of the Sea* – points
to the mid-eighteenth century as the moment when France ceased to
experience the coast and shoreline as a territory to fear; instead it became
a pleasurable recreation area. Paintings such as those by by Adriaen van
de Velde indicate that in the Netherlands the pleasures and delights of
the seashore life had been discovered at least a hundred years earlier.
There are, notwithstanding, differences between the seventeenth- and
nineteenth-century Netherlandish visions of the coastal scene. In the
monumental beach scene by Jan Hendrik Weissenbruch from 1887, *p. 101*
human beings are indeed present: but their presence serves merely to
accentuate for the spectator the vastness of the open sea, the immensity
beyond the Netherlandish coast. They intensify our experience of the
sublime as we view this seascape of clouds, sea, ships and shore.
The horizon is low and the five small anonymous figures beneath it,
with a miniscule dog, appear to serve as colour accents. It is as if
nature has grown far too large for them. Spectators can easily identify
with figures in the painting whose backs are towards them; they are
anonymous and, like the spectator, facing towards the landscape.
Through them we experience our own insignificance in the face of the
overwhelming vastness of the heavens above us and the earth beneath.
This was the sense of nature which the romantics before Weissenbruch
had discovered. And whether you find yourself in the mountain heights
or on the shoreless sea, ever since the romantics it has been impossible
to colonize nature with impunity.
There are of course also panoramic views which aim to provide an
overwhelming experience of nature without introducing human
figures to provide a sense of scale and to stress the insignificance of the
individual. One of the most impressive examples of this is the painting
by Jan Toorop showing the sea near the Dutch seaside town of Katwijk. *p. 103*
The confrontation with the foaming tops of the breaking waves is so
immediate and so powerful that you feel as if you are being drenched in
the strong salty wetness. This time it is the painted sea that reminds you
of your insignificance in comparison with the forces of nature. No human
figures are needed.

Intimacy and Serenity

The period 1750–1850 tends to be neglected in the history of Netherlandish landscape painting. In the exhibition 'The Discovery of the Netherlands' these years are significant not so much because many new regions were discovered by painters in this country but more importantly because in this period, far more than before, landscape paintings presented scenes emanating peace and tranquillity. A good example of this is Jacob van Strij's painting of the river landscape near Dordrecht. *p. 77* Certain seventeenth-century Dutch masters such as Jan van Goyen and Albert Cuyp had long ago revealed the beauty of the city of Dordrecht and its surrounding countryside. But Van Strij brings to this world a remarkable sense of tranquillity. This is achieved through the clear light, through the still waters, through the meticulous rendering of the leaves on the trees, both nearby and in the distance. Above all it is the light: in this painting it gleams through a doorway in a fence on the righthand side, streams through the fencing, dances between the trees, glances upon a wall. Possibly we should not call this great art and it is easy to detect stylistic borrowings from the master Albert Cuyp in Van Strij's work. But there is no question of Van Strij's skill in creating a landscape from which emanates a remarkable intimacy and serenity, something that is characteristic of many landscape paintings of his period.

For me, the most moving record of the yearning after an intimate landscape is the *Bleaching Field beside a Brook in Gelderland*, painted by Wouter van Troostwijk in around 1809. He is one of the great artists who *p. 75* did not live long enough for his work to make any substantial impact upon the painting of his time. Only a few pieces by him have survived – but each one, without exception, is a masterpiece. What makes this picture of a bleaching field utterly unforgettable is the way it combines total informality with an astonishingly bold presentation of what at first sight appears to be a randomly-chosen insignificant small meadow. Edward Norgate, writing in the 1620s, already described the artist as a creator of the schemata which then go on to serve as moulds for our experience of nature's beauty. Artists also require fixed organizational principles in order to suggest a three-dimensional reality when painting on a flat surface. But in this case it seems as if Van Troostwijk decided to relinquish any attempt at schematization.

Untrammelled, authoritatively, he looks about him and then selects, apparently at random, a small patch of countryside which he makes the subject of his painting. Only after a while do you notice how subtly he is working – how the placing of the tree beside the stream and the two figures bring depth into his picture. But it is chiefly the suggestion that this reflects an authentic experience of being out in the country and enjoying nature that urges us to accept the picture as a landscape that actually exists. This intimate corner of the province of Gelderland glows into life also because Van Troostwijk is a painter with an enormous understanding of the plastic presence of groups of trees. The cottage under the trees seems sculpted out of the paint and this gives it an almost monumental presence in the picture. And then there is all the thickly-painted rich green of grass and leaves. It is clear from this work that the artist is concerned with an individual interpretation of the landscape scene, with the way in which the painter can reproduce an unpretentious piece of countryside and transform it into a vision offering intense delight. In this way Van Troostwijk introduced a most important renewal into nineteenth-century landscape art.

As a young man, Andreas Schelfhout – especially in his early work – also invites the viewer to share his intimate experience of nature. But his style of painting is very different. Around 1825–1830 he made an oil sketch on paper showing a farmhouse near The Hague; it is structured into areas of p. 81 colour with zones of bright light through which he creates space in front of and behind the trees. Schelfhout lays on his paint far more thinly than Van Troostwijk. He renders trees and leaves with a draughtsman's meticulousness. But the overall effect is attractively informal. It is as if, quite by chance, you experience a moment in which you realize that beauty is revealed to those who notice the unobtrusive, the unpretentious. Here again there is a figure seen from behind, who leads us into this intimate world. Indeed, Wouter van Troostwijk and Andreas Schelfhout have revealed to us the intimacy of our own countryside. This profound relationship with the landscape is expressed quite literally in Matthijs Maris's work from 1860, *The Origin*. In this work the viewer's gaze is p. 67 drawn into the earth, into the source.

Come Rain or Shine
In seventeenth-century paintings the weather often appears underspecified. In the winter scenes of Hendrick Avercamp, for instance, it doesn't seem to be really cold. The primary function of the ice is to provide a seasonal basis for recreation! One of the first artists who succeeded in capturing actual weather conditions and rendering them in painting was Jan van Goyen. His *View of Dordrecht from Papendrecht* p. 43

(1633) presents a convincing picture of a turbulent river Merwede, the waters roughened by a strong breeze and illuminated by rays of sunlight that break through the clouds at irregular intervals. It gives a highly recognizable picture of an all-too-familiar type of Dutch weather. In 1989 a large exhibition was mounted in Amsterdam's Rijksmuseum on the topic of landscape art. It was suggested that Dutch TV weather forecaster Erwin Krol should be asked to give a weather prediction based on the painting by Jacob van Ruisdael, *The Windmill at Wijk bij Duurstede*. It turned out to be impossible. According to Krol, Ruisdael had jumbled up three different weather types in his painting. It was easy enough to explain why this had happened: seventeenth-century painters were used to working in studios, not outdoors; so weather conditions were not copied from reality. Again, Ruisdael did not position himself on one spot outdoors to paint his picture of the windmill. Instead, he composed the landscape from various sketches and created an imposing cloud-filled sky above. Maybe Ruisdael's clouds fail to convince a modern meteorologist but for centuries the ordinary spectator has been so impressed by his work that in Dutch the expression 'a Ruisdael sky' is commonly used. Netherlanders use the term when referring both to paintings as well as the reality of billowing cumuli.

Not until the early nineteenth century did meteorological research make it possible to predict the weather by understanding the significance of cloud patterns. Thereafter, the sky acquired a new meaning: beside the spiritual sense of 'the heavens' and its role in creating a certain mood in paintings, it gained a more realistic content. The English painter Constable was well aware that the clouds and skies in his paintings should be 'true to nature'. So out he went in all weathers, armed with his sketchbook, and painted the sky, duly noting down the time of day, the date and the type of weather he observed. Slowly but surely his example was followed elsewhere. If there is one thing for which we should be grateful to the painters of The Hague School, then it is that they have taken the weather in the Netherlands and promoted it to chief topic in their works. In 1884 Paul Gabriël, like Ruisdael, also painted a mill – not in Wijk bij Duurstede, but in the polder of the Leidschedam, near The Hague. And in this *p. 97* case you may happily call in weatherman Erwin Krol. It seems unlikely, however, that Gabriël would have painted such a huge picture outdoors. Probably he made preliminary studies in watercolour of the weather conditions in this polder and then created the painting back in his studio. It is widely accepted that the French impressionists were the ones who introduced a sense of mood and atmosphere into landscape painting. This may well be so, but it often amounts to the obligatory carefree mood experienced in a *vie des vacances*. The Netherlandish impressionists, on the other hand, were famed in Europe and the United States for the sensitivity with which they portrayed many different weather conditions. It is shameful to relate, but in the Netherlands for about a century we disregarded the international reputation of the painters of The Hague School and were scarcely aware that many of their best works had found their way into collections abroad. The art museums of Boston, Glasgow, Munich and Moscow contain the most superb works by Jozef Israëls, Anton Mauve, the Maris brothers and their contemporaries. One of these paintings, Mauve's *A Dutch Road*, is presently in Toledo (Ohio). What is exceptional about it is that it can be regarded as the wettest painting in the history of Netherlandish art.

p. 93

In 1880 Anton Mauve, painting in the Gooi region of lakes and woodland, recorded a country road along which a farmer is riding with three horses. Actually, it is quite inaccurate to say 'riding' – it is more like squelchy trudging through soggy marshland. The sky is grey, scarcely a leaf still hangs upon the trees, the ditches are full to overflowing and the unpaved road is a mass of puddles. But this sombre scene has inspired the artist to compose one of the most beautiful symphonies of subtle greys that I have ever seen.

Fifteen years later Floris Verster gazed across the snow-covered landscape of South Holland and was inspired to compose his delicious painting *Snowy Landscape*. The market gardens in the Leiden district are illuminated by a mellow red evening sun against which the bare trees appear like calligraphy. Indeed, you could describe the work as an icon of winter. With paintings like these, artists have opened our eyes to the wonders of nature in all kinds of weather.

p. 105

The Landscape and the Soul of the People

In the Gemeentemuseum in The Hague there is a large painting by Jacob Maris from 1878 depicting what in English would be called allotment patches, where city dwellers without gardens may grow their flowers and vegetables. This seems a somewhat uninteresting subject and was painted in the most dismal weather conditions. What makes an artist depict something like this? Is it in order to show that he can transform into art absolutely any corner of the world, whatever the weather? Certainly. But there is something else too. He must also be convinced that reproducing

p. 91

what is unquestionablty picturesque in nature is an inadequate means of conveying the essential character of his country. It is as if this painting announces demonstratively that pre-planned renderings of the landscape fail: the beauty they deliver is only artifical.

The conscious quest in search of that which is typical of one's own country, including all the discomforts, the ideology of the anti-archaic and the anti-schematic was first formulated by the distinguished German art historian and jurist Karl Schnaase, who published the famous *Niederländische Briefe* (Letters from the Netherlands) in 1834 after his visit to the Mauritshuis. Later he read these letters to art students at the Art Academy in Düsseldorf, at that time the major centre in Europe for new ideas on landscape painting. Gazing at works by Dutch seventeenth-century masters in a Dutch museum Schnaase realized that the task of the artist is to make people aware of what is uniquely characteristic of the landscape. That unique quality gained a far deeper significance in his writings than had previously been the case among artists and art historians. It was not simply a question of outward 'visible forms' but what shape, or physical appearance did Nature adopt in order to express her inner, essential spirit. As Schnaase put it, '*in welcher Gestalt spricht die Natur den ihr inwohnende Geist physionomisch aus?*'

According to Schnaase, nature determines not only the lives of farmers and shepherds but those of every single person in a given country: their lives are shaped by the nature in their land, and that makes them who they are. If you want to know what life is really like in a country, you have to understand the idiosyncrasies of that land's climate. It's no good simply making hay while the sun shines in Arcadia! You need to understand the hardships, the animosities of a landscape, the pitiless peltings of rain and hail, the merciless beating of the noonday sun, because people are deeply affected by the landscapes in which they live. The landscape around them penetrates, as it were, into a person's entire being and shapes the character of a people: '*das ganze geistige Wesen des Volks, wie das Blut den Körper, und wird so zum Volkskarakter*'. This is the earliest echo of the idea about the connection between a nation, or a people, and their natural environment – the *Blut und Boden* or Blood and Soil notion. It was to resonate down the whole of the nineteenth century and into the twentieth.

A landscape artist should aim to present the physiognomy of nature and in order to do this must penetrate into the 'soul of the people' which is expressed through the natural surroundings in which it is nourished.

It goes without saying that when Jacob Maris sat painting some allotment plots on a drizzly day he was not pondering on points of Hegelian philosophy over which Schnaase had theorized. But the notion that the landscape was a metaphor for a people, a nation, had in Maris's world become generally accepted. The climate, the type of soil, the crops that were produced – all these contributed to the character of the local people, to their 'nature'.

The Personal Landscape

The idea of a national landscape that had become widespread partly due to Schnaase's writings was replaced towards the close of the nineteenth century by the notion of art as the extremely personal interpretation of each single artist. Jan Voerman paints the river polders and the Dutch cows but these are seen as his personal vision. Indeed, his art became his life. After a period in Amsterdam he left the city for the countryside and withdrew to the small town of Hattem, near where he was born. He painted the surrounding landscape, where the river IJssel flows quietly *p. 107* by; moments caught in time, an endless series of scenes full of light, sky and water.

At almost the same time Vincent van Gogh was painting his landscapes in France. From 1892 on they were exhibited in the Netherlands and they demonstrated that the private universe of one artist could extend far beyond the individual rendering or reality, indeed, that the landscape could express the feelings of the artist. And this caused a quiet landslide in the Dutch landscape. Painters such as Mondrian, Sluijters, and Altink were all slightly infected by Van Gogh's vision. Sluijters's picture *Moonlit Night* is painted near the pretty town of Laren, but it appears to be an *p. 113* excuse to compose a symphony of blues, reds and purples. And in a similar way Mondrian uses the landscape like a draftsman's board – upon which he can learn about line, depth and proportion. Now we are not so much seeing the landscape through the eyes of the artist – we are looking into the artist's soul.

The Lost Landcape

In Amsterdam's Rijksmuseum there is a charming and surprisingly modern-looking work by the Dutch nineteenth-century painter Charles Rochussen. He painted it to commemorate the opening of the Scheveningen racecourse on 3 August 1846. The small painting greets *p. 83* us like a jaunty, cheerful reportage. But the scene it shows no longer exists. The empty fields have been filled. The church and the nearby pavilion Von Wied (now the sculpture museum Beelden aan Zee) are now overshadowed by huge highrises. This little world, lying between the streets Gevers Deynootweg, Badhuisweg and Stevensstraat is now an uninterrupted mess of buildings and counts as one of the most spectacular failures in the history of Dutch urban planning. What the painting records is a landcape that is lost forever.

The Musée des Augustins in Toulouse contains a small painting by the eighteenth-century artist Paulus La Fargue from The Hague. It is the pendant of another small painting in The Hague Historical Museum. Both pictures show people taking a walk along the street Rijswijkseweg and the small street Bocht van Guinea – today in The Hague's centre. *p. 65, 67* Once upon a time, life flowed gently along these streets; now the traffic screeches past rows of apartment dwellings. Another striking example of a lost landscape is Jacob van Ruisdael's painting *The Kostverloren House* made in the seventeenth century. He depicts the beautiful polder *p. 55* landscape beside the river Amstel, which so delighted Rembrandt on his walks round Amsterdam. Only small stretches of this scenery remain, surrounded by suburbs and dominated by the ever-visible Ajax football stadium.

Sometimes it is illuminating to look at photographs and see the contrast between today's scene and the painted landscape of bygone times. Undoubtedly this offers striking images – something which became clear

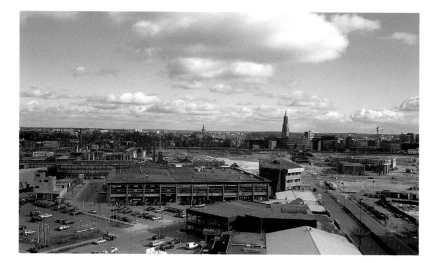

to me when I was looking at a photograph of the view of Amersfoort taken from the same place as where Withoos made the drawings for his cityscapes. So there is every reason to lament the urban sprawl that is defiling the Dutch landscape. But we decided it was rather an obvious way of striving for effect to place a modern photograph beside the old painting. Over the past three centuries the Netherlands' population has increased more than sevenfold. Rather than lamenting what this has meant in terms of reduction of open spaces, the unprejudiced rambler is still quite capable of enjoying the countryside – where, thanks to careful planning, much has been preserved. In any case, the sprawl has not encroached to such an extent that the aesthetic reclamation of the Netherlands by artists of former times has become totally unrecognizable. Bygone artists have portrayed the beauties of our land and we can still delight in them to this day.

In conclusion

If you are to select a mere forty landscape paintings from the thousands available, you need to know what you are looking for. And for that you need experts. It requires intensive discussion to hammer out the requirements, so that you avoid making arbitrary choices. Huigen Leeflang and Jenny Reynaerts were the very experts I needed. I discovered that 'proletarian shopping' with Huigen and Jenny – that is, choosing the most wonderful works and without paying a penny carrying them off for our exhibition – was a far richer experience than doing this on one's own. Carin Reinders, the director of Apeldoorn's CODA, a museum and centre for contemporary art and local history, inspired us with her enthusiasm and created an atmosphere in which the 'discovery of the Netherlands' became a voyage of adventure which I shall not easily forget.

A Landscape with a Down-to-Earth Flavour

Louise O. Fresco

The Netherlands that acquires its contours through Henk van Os's voyage of discovery is a unique place. It is not a country full of dramatic rocky formations, desolate plains, wild rivers or impenetrable coniferous forests. Here and there, such as in Jan van Goyen's *View of Haarlem and the Haarlemmer Meer*, the low horizon and the great feeling of spaciousness created by this flat landscape make man diminutive, but nowhere is he insignificant: the two female farm labourers taking a rest from their work are totally in proportion to the polder they are overlooking. Other paintings, such as Paul Gabriël's *Watermill near the Leidschedam*, break the loftiness of the sky with unmistakable signs of human activity in the form of cows, and above all, the windmill that towers majestically over the landscape. In the same way, the vertical white surface of the front facade in *The Kostverloren House on the Amstel near Amsterdam* by Jacob Ruisdael is the dominant element. Yet other paintings show the presence of human beings tied in with the intimacy of the landscape, such as Meindert Hobbema's *Watermill at Singraven near Denekamp* or Joris van der Haagens *Panorama near Arnhem*.

Without exception, the paintings included in the selection for 'The Discovery of the Netherlands' radiate serenity and self-assurance. They depict an unthreatening landscape, where the trees often remain unruffled by the wind and the sunlight falls in parallel streaks creating intimate vistas, as in the *Farmyard* by Andreas Schelfhout, where we are looking at the open clearing in the wood in the same way as the human figure in the foreground. This is a place where people can travel around the countryside without fear or trepidation and where the town is never far away, as in the early work by Esaias van de Velde, *Dune Landscape with Horsemen* from 1614. Even in Jan Hendrik Weissenbruch's beach scene, cited by Henk van Os in his essay, the people provide an indication of the scale so that we can 'experience the vast panorama . . . even more intensely'. The magnitude of the scenery is in no way disquieting. The scale is merely relative. The predominantly green fields and abundance of trees reflect the fertile soil. Landscape and town are closely interconnected, as in *Rope-Walk 'de kleingarenbaan' in Gouda* by Joris Herst, where just over the fence we can again see cows grazing in the meadow, or in Paulus La Fargue's *Rijswijkseweg* from 1772, where the road is bordered on one side by houses and on the other by a meadow with its horse and chickens. Even in townscapes the agrarian element is always close at hand, as can be seen in the Hendrick ten Oever's painting providing a view of Amersfoort, where in addition to the bathers there are cows standing quite unperturbed.

The Netherlands seen here is a place inhabited by people who know they seldom have to fear the natural environment and more likely than not dominate it themselves, because to a large extent the landscape itself has been created by human hands. In such man-made scenery, the farmer with his farmhouse and animals is unlikely to be very far away. We see farmsteads and houses, dikes and ditches, horses, cows and sheep, trees that have been planted by man and well-tended pastures. The fields are divided up into variegated strips of green, proof that this is a countryside of human dimensions. A land of water and sky, how could it be otherwise, but specifically of functional water: drainage ditches, canals and rivers, which once were used for transporting goods. This is beautifully illustrated in *Mills at Giethoorn* by Willem Bastiaan Tholen, where a small, narrow bridge over a ditch has been singled out, giving perspective to the two small walking figures in the foreground, who otherwise would have appeared insignificant beside the dominant windmills. In a countryside of human dimensions everything is well-disposed towards man. The skies are lofty but not overpowering, filled with clouds that are more likely to presage a drizzle than to augur a storm; this is even the case in Jan Voerman's painting *Moving Sky*. Only in *A Dutch Road* by Anton Mauve is it raining lightly, but there, too, we can see that behind the clouds the sun – still low in the sky – is gathering strength. Proudly, the towers in *View of Amersfoort* by Matthias Withoos rise above the landscape, while the houses and farmlands are bathing in soft light. The sea too, our arch-enemy, is almost always calm, as are the rivers. In Johan Conrad Greives *Bombproof Rampart at Vlissingen*, the only threatening element is the garrison itself and possibly the prow of the large fishing boat on the foreshore, but not the tranquil, shimmering surface of the sea. And even in the painting where the threat of flooding is perceptible, the dramatic *Inundation* by Hendrik Chabot, it is once again the farmhouses that dominate and provide the central theme and not the forces of nature. The only painting in which man is truly absent is Jan Toorop's *Sea at Katwijk*, where we see only waves. Nevertheless even this sea conveys the idea of an unruffled rather than a hostile presence.

Thus the landscape of the Netherlands that we find by following Henk van Os's voyage of discovery is, almost without exception, agricultural and rural.[1] It is in the first place developing, as time goes by, into a landscape of towns closely interacting with the countryside. Even when the process of urbanization started to pick up speed towards the end of the

1
The seascapes might be an exception, were it not for the fact that the official international definition of 'agriculture and agrarian' also covers fishery.

eighteenth century, the rural character was almost universally retained, and this continued to be the case until far into the twentieth century.

In *The Veere Fishing Fleet* by Jan Toorop, much of the painting is taken up by agricultural fields. And everywhere – once again with the exception of the painting by Toorop, *Sea at Katwijk* mentioned earlier – the landscape is one of human making. In one painting, *Peatery* (1650) by Jacob Sibrandi Mancadan, this human interference is even the subject of the work. Sometimes there is a clear reference to man in the landscape even if the landscape itself is the subject of the painting: to the left in the *View at Eext* by Egbert van Drielst, if we look carefully, we see two cottages with pigs rooting around in the dirt outside, and even a ladder propped up against a tree – all partially screened by high trees in the woods. Sometimes this reference is concealed from the observer. Sometimes man is ostensibly absent, as in the painting *The Origin (Forest View near Oosterbeek)* (1860) by Matthijs Maris, where we can see a wild stretch of woodland on a slope. Nonetheless, for a Dutch landscape expert there can be no doubt: this is not unsullied countryside. These woods are susceptible to erosion: the tree-roots have become exposed as the earth has been washed away, the fertile leaf mould has been partly dug up, trees have been chopped down and the logs transported elsewhere. And even the beach scenes and seascapes are not entirely unspoilt, because from early times onwards man has been planting seagrass; as well as protecting and making use of beaches and dunes (which can be seen beautifully in the way the beach has been ploughed up in the painting *Racecourse at Scheveningen* by Charles Rochussen).

This voyage of discovery through the Netherlands shows us cultivated landscapes, as opposed to untouched nature. More than in any other country the landscape in the Netherlands is the product of human achievement, of conquering and transforming natural ecosystems to ensure the survival of man. *God created the world, but the Dutch created the Netherlands*. The primeval vegetation of the Netherlands was a dense, temperate deciduous forest, featuring oaks, limes, ashes, elms and beeches. These tree species established themselves in our country from the end of the last ice age (thus from about 9000 years ago). In ecological terms this is of course a very recent type of vegetation.

This primeval forest is not to be seen in one single painting, the only reminders of what once must have been a forest are a couple of old oaks, or a clump of trees here and there. The reason for the disappearance of forest areas is the practice of arable farming. From pollen research[2] we

2
We know this mainly through the proportional relation between the seeds of graminaceous and tree species, which show a strong prevalence in favour of trees, even in wetter parts, which are now sometimes seen as 'natural' pastures.

know that the original forest started to disappear gradually 5000 years ago, due to the cutting down of trees to make clearings where they could lay out fields and meadows. If the farmer temporarily abandoned the land and the cattle also disappeared from the meadows, the forest regained the land spontaneously. However, as time went on, using the forest for pasture led to cattle grazing on young seedlings and trampling them down – making regrowth increasingly unlikely. The end result was park landscapes, dotted by vestiges of the old forest. When this land was used even more intensively, the park landscape was downgraded to grassland and moors, particularly in the case of wet and sandy ground (where large sand drifts were even known to occur). This intensified use of the land involved not only grazing, cutting down trees and reeds, but also making use of the forest's upper layer of fertile soil – and using the top layer of the moors to enrich farmland elsewhere, thus creating in traditionally Dutch style the typically high-lying *essen* or *engen*. This diverse, open landscape with park-like areas, fertile fields, pasture and moorland is home to a great wealth of flora and fauna. To put it more irreverently, this biological diversity is an unintentional by-product of agriculture. Thus farming, and use of land and water (for instance for peat cutting and water drainage) has generally created a number of new ecological habitats for plants and animals. This ecological by-product of great aesthetic value is the landscape seen in 'The Discovery of the Netherlands'.[3]

What the painters in 'The Discovery of the Netherlands' show us is a deeply rural and agricultural landscape of human dimensions, an unthreatening, park-like decor where man is not reduced to a mere nonentity, but is connected to everything around him. It is these landscapes in particular (the area dominated by the great rivers such as the Rhine tributaries with their wide lines of view, the tranquil moors and the pleasant stream valleys) that have been the focus of emerging nature conservancy from the early twentieth century. It is striking how often rural and 'natural' landscapes were painted in the course of the nineteenth century, just when urbanization was bringing about unmistakable change on an unprecedented scale. However, it is impossible to validate whether this was actually happening more than it had in the past, since we are only dealing with a selection of the paintings produced at that time.[4] Nonetheless, a number of prominent landscapes in which the agricultural and rural elements are important date from the nineteenth and early twentieth centuries, starting with Wouter van Troostwijk's *Bleaching Field beside a Brook in Gelderland* (1805-1810) through to Floris Verster's

3
Since the 1980s intensive research has been carried out into the evolution of the landscape in the Netherlands. The procedures described above are of course much too simple, because the succession of grass and shrubs and woods is being continuously repeated (and for instance is influenced by birds and large grazers spreading seeds) and is not exclusively determined by agriculture. However, the important thing here is that our perception of the role of agriculture and land utilization by man in general is decisive in the vision of what the natural environment is.

4
When this article was being written the definitive list of works for the exhibition had not yet been finalized, so it was not possible to really make quantitative judgments about the proportion of rural to non-rural paintings.

Snowy Landscape with his pollard willows and fruit trees from 1895, and tailing off with *Red Farm* (1924) by Jan Altink.
With these works the landscape painters have given the obvious qualities of rural landscape a beauty all its own. Thus they are preparing the way for a new awareness of the landscape as something that should be conserved. They were the template makers, as Henk van Os says: they literally put a frame around the natural environment, they allowed us not only to experience the beauty of nature, but also presented it to us as being of value in its own right; and as with everything of value it must be protected. The late nineteenth century and early twentieth century are the seminal years for nature conservancy in which Jac. P. Thijsse and Eli Heimans were the founding fathers of the oldest organizations in this field: The Society for the Preservation of Nature Monuments in the Netherlands and The Royal Dutch Society for the Study of Wildlife. This marked the beginning of the concept of 'nature management' or 'nature conservancy'. Thijsse and Heimans were originally ornithologists and their concern for the countryside was prompted in the first place by the desire to protect birds' nesting grounds. For a large part these areas were to be found at the margins of agricultural domains, as on the island of Texel (where Thijsse worked for a few years) and in the Naardermeer. However, it soon became clear that not only the rugged, ostensibly vacant countryside had to be protected,[5] but more urgently the transitional areas between agriculture and wild grassland, between woods and pasturage, between moorland and stream valley. They are all to be found in that typical Dutch park landscape that accommodates a great diversity of species due to its ecology of gradual transition from wet to dry, fertile to infertile, brackish to freshwater, protected from or exposed to the winds. In the course of the twentieth century the concept of 'nature conservancy' has been further developed and refined. Not only was the countryside to be protected, but where it had already disappeared, a policy of reintroduction was to be pursued, showing that we can consciously cultivate natural environments and design them according to given criteria. Moreover, criticism of the role of agriculture as destroyer of natural beauty and values grew. From the early twentieth century many of these man-made landscapes disappeared due to increases in scale, intensification and rationalization in farming – a process which reached its climax in terms of land reform and consolidation in the land consolidation that took place in the 1970s. That created a remarkable and in a sense tragic paradox: the same type of agriculture that was largely responsible

5
As pointed out above, almost the entire natural environment was also subject to human influence, even the Naardermeer, although that was not known at the time.

for the creation of desired man-made landscapes was also capable of destroying them. This started a heated discussion which is still going on today about what the original landscape of the Netherlands actually was: do large grazers and fallow deer belong in it and are coniferous trees part of it (which originally – at least after the last ice age – were not to be found in the Netherlands)? Can and should agriculture play a role in the preservation of the landscape? The latter has become widely accepted now the 'ecological services' of agriculture are recognized and remunerated by the European Union.

And how will our views of the natural environment develop from here? According to a recent survey, young people think the countryside is boring. Woods and moors are at best a place to enjoy motocross rallies and, at a pinch, a city park can find favour in their eyes as a meeting point.[6] Others commend the increase in the number of golf courses as a blessing for the countryside. They are not represented in paintings yet, but one day I would like to see the landscapes of 'The Discovery of the Netherlands of the Twenty-First Century'. It would be interesting because, to adapt a citation from Simon Schama,[7] a landscape is a canvas on which we project our obsessions and ideals about nature . The landscape painters supply the forms, both now and in the future.

How we are to assess original nature will always be a pivotal question for conservationists. Ecologists are divided on the question. Almost the entire Dutch population feels that the beauty of nature is similar to a small-scale agricultural landscape, with alternating high and low vegetation, copses and woods. That is the ideal image that is endorsed time and time again in surveys. The Dutch want to see cows in the meadow, with pollard willows for decoration and thatched farmhouses, with here and there an area with sand drifts and flourishing moorland. That is the image that has become planted in our collective memory, largely due to our landscape painters.

That image stretches back farther than the emergence of the nature conservancy movement. From the time of Hendrik ten Oever's *View of Zwolle* from 1675, our dominant image has been that of the Arcadian agrarian landscape that emanates tranquillity and self-reliance, where in the intrinsically warm atmosphere of cows, trees and farmsteads people feel secure because nature is well-disposed towards them. And because in the Netherlands, whether we are talking about the landscape or anything else, in the end the human measure is the measure of all things.

6
Research by the Dutch Forestry Commission, whereby it is striking to note that immigrant youths (of Moroccan and Turkish descent) appreciate woods even less than youths from the indigenous population, but they appreciate open agrarian landscapes rather more.

7
In Landscape and Memory *(New York: Vintage Books, 1995) Schama calls a landscape 'a text on which generations write their recurring obsessions'.*

Catalogue

Lenders to the exhibition

Amsterdam Historical Museum, Amsterdam
Caldic Collectie BV, Rotterdam
Centraal Museum, Utrecht
Chabot Museum, Rotterdam
Dordrechts Museum, Dordrecht
Drents Museum, Assen
Gemeentemuseum Den Haag, The Hague
Groninger Museum, Groningen
Haags Historisch Museum, The Hague
Kröller-Müller Museum, Otterlo
Royal Cabinet of Paintings Mauritshuis, The Hague
Metropolitan Museum of Art, New York
Musée des Augustins, Toulouse
Museum Flehite, Amersfoort
MuseumgoudA, Gouda
Museum van Loon, Amsterdam
National Gallery, London
Private collections from the Netherlands and Belgium
Rijksmuseum Amsterdam, Amsterdam
Rijksmuseum Twenthe, Enschede
Stedelijk Museum, Kampen
Talbot Rice Gallery of Art at The University of Edinburgh
Teylers Museum, Haarlem
Toledo Museum of Art, Toledo (Ohio)

Hendrick Avercamp, *Winter Scene outside the Walls of Kampen*, 1613–1615
panel, 44.5 x 72.5 cm
Private collection

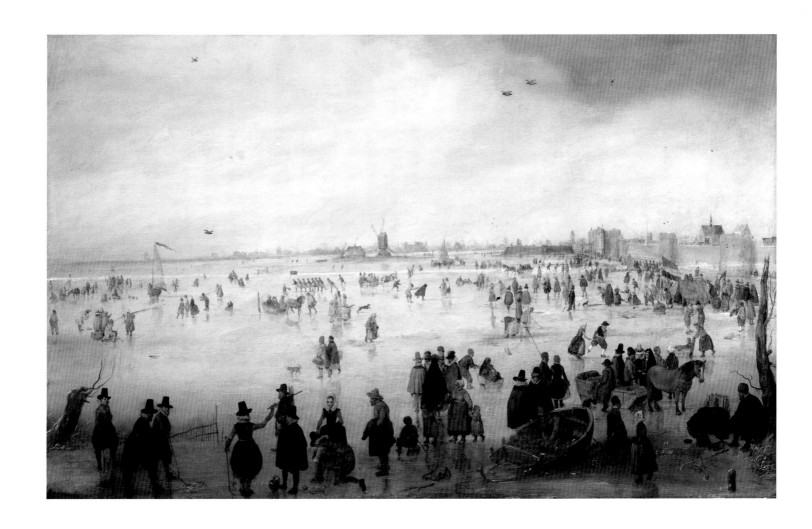

Esaias van de Velde, *Dune Landscape with Horsemen*, 1614
panel, 25 x 33 cm
Rijksmuseum Twente, Enschede

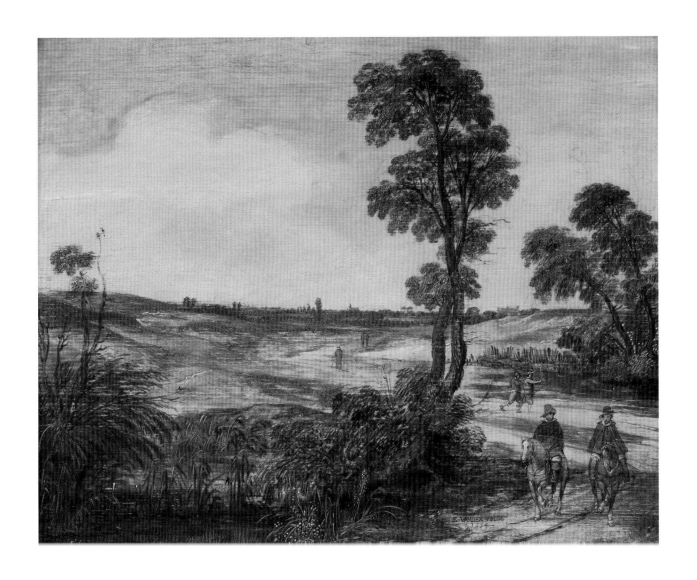

Jan Josefsz. van Goyen, *View of Dordrecht from Papendrecht*, 1633
panel, 47 x 73 cm
Royal Cabinet of Paintings Mauritshuis, The Hague

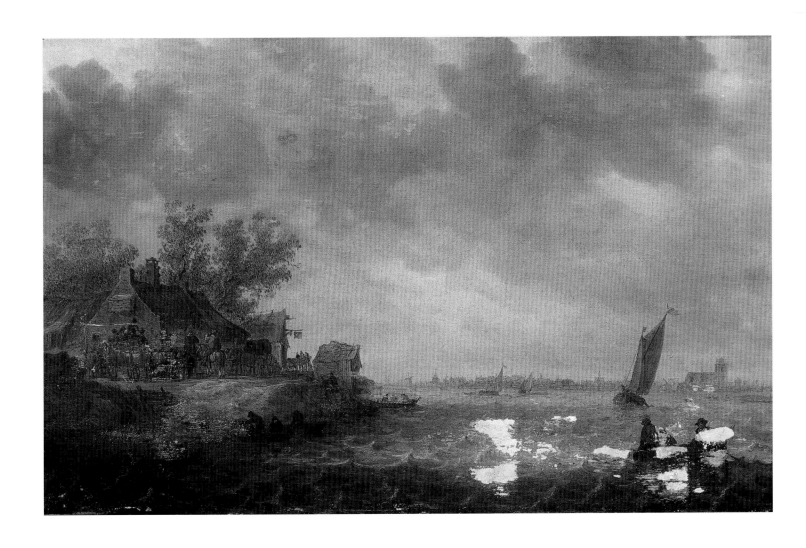

Jan Josefsz. van Goyen, *View of Haarlem and the Haarlemmer Meer*, 1646
panel, 34.6 x 50.5 cm
The Metropolitan Museum of Art, New York
Purchase, 1871 (71.62)

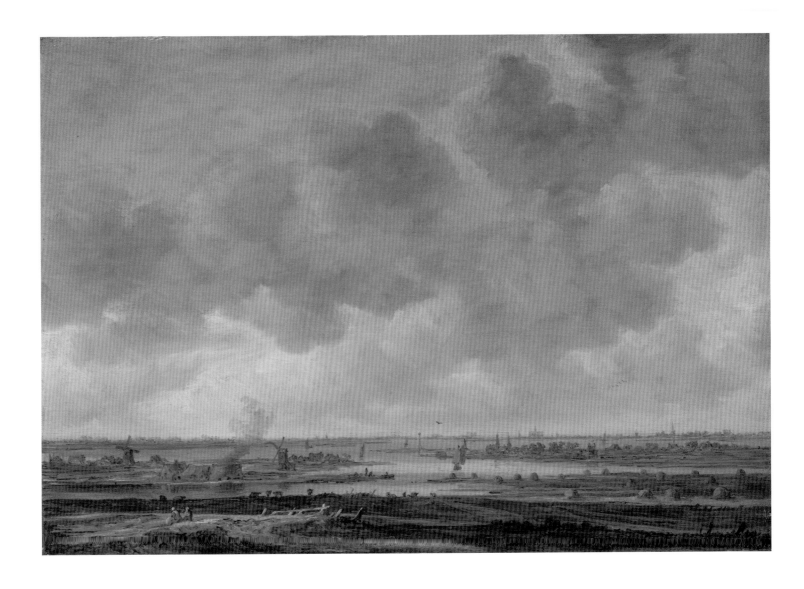

Joris van der Haagen, *Panorama near Arnhem* (left),1649
canvas, 66 x 89 cm
Royal Cabinet of Paintings Mauritshuis, The Hague

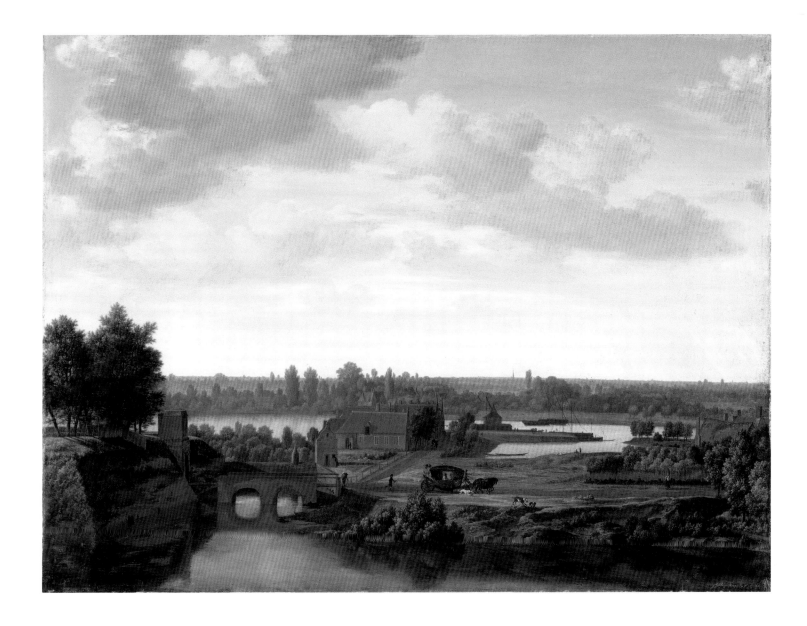

Joris van der Haagen, *Panorama near Arnhem* (right), 1649
canvas, 66 x 89 cm
Royal Cabinet of Paintings Mauritshuis, The Hague

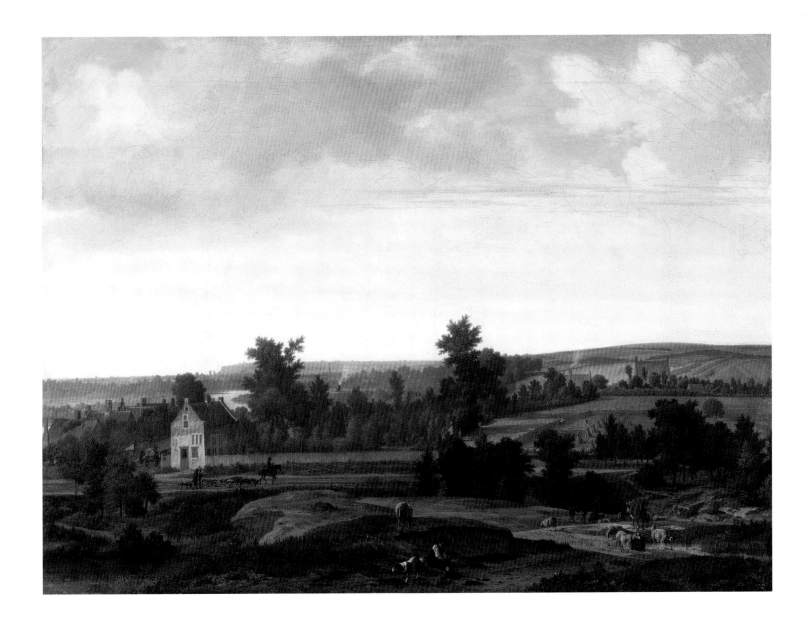

49

Aert van der Neer, *Moonlit Landscape*, 1650
panel, 74 x 68 cm
Dordrechts Museum, Dordrecht

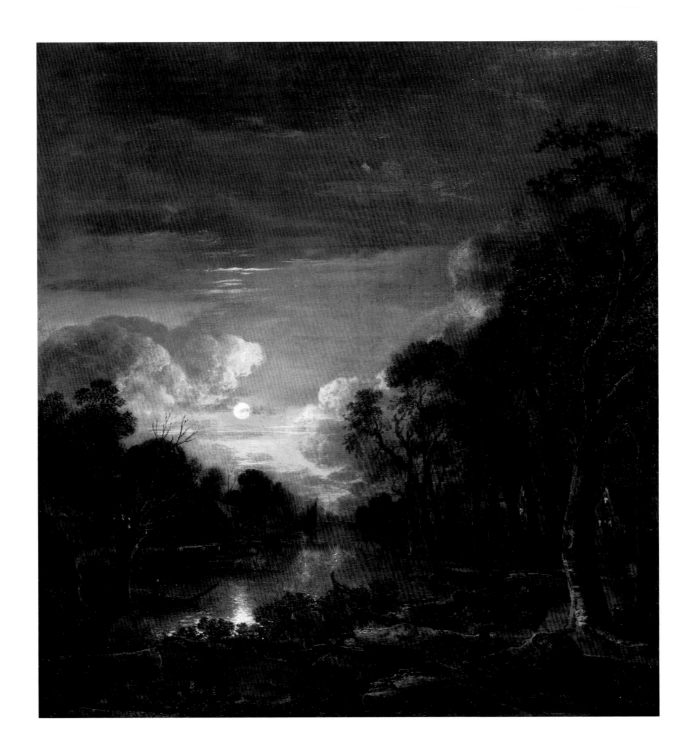

Jacob Sibrandi Mancadan, *Peatery*, 1650
canvas, 131 x 182 cm
Groninger Museum, Groningen
On loan from Stichting de Ploeg, Groningen

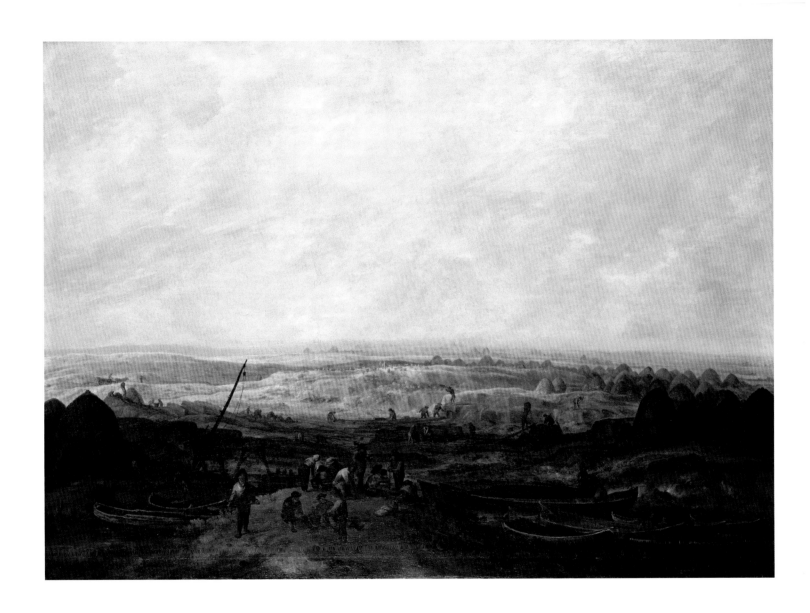

Jacob Isaacksz. van Ruisdael, *The Kostverloren House on the Amstel near Amsterdam*, c. 1660
canvas, 96 x 108 cm
Amsterdam Historical Museum, Amsterdam
Acquired with assistance from the Vereniging Rembrandt

I float along your crystal ways,
Borne upon your silver tide.
In my fleet water coach I glide,
seeking new pleasures for my eyes.
My Amstel stream flowing sweetly by,
Your lovely vistas can supply
Bright jewels for my poetry.
My soul exults in liberty.

Nicolaas Simon van Winter

Nicolaas Simon van Winter
(1718–1795), from:
*De Amstelstroom, in zes
zangen* (Amsterdam, 1755).

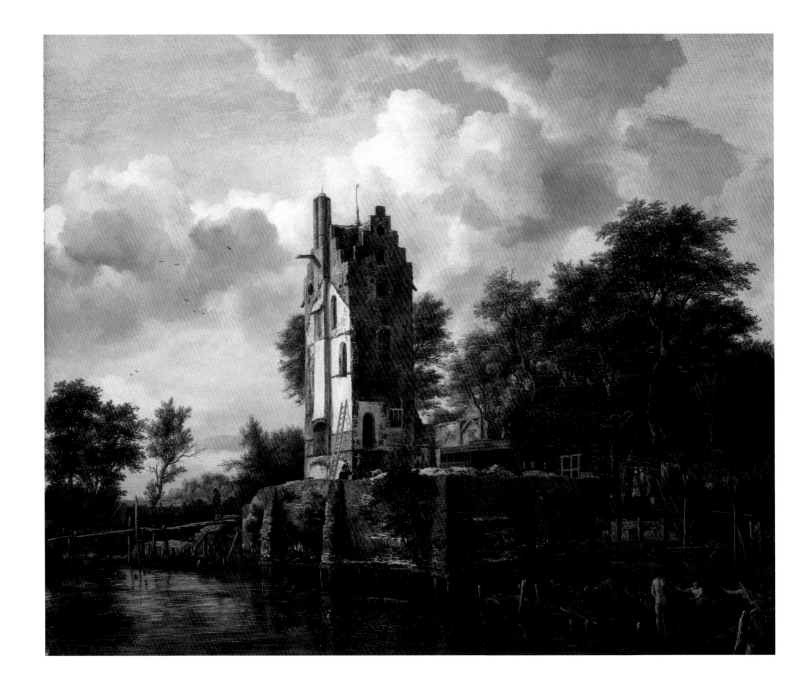

Adriaen van de Velde, *Beach View*, 1663–1665
panel, 42 x 54 cm
Royal Cabinet of Paintings Mauritshuis, The Hague

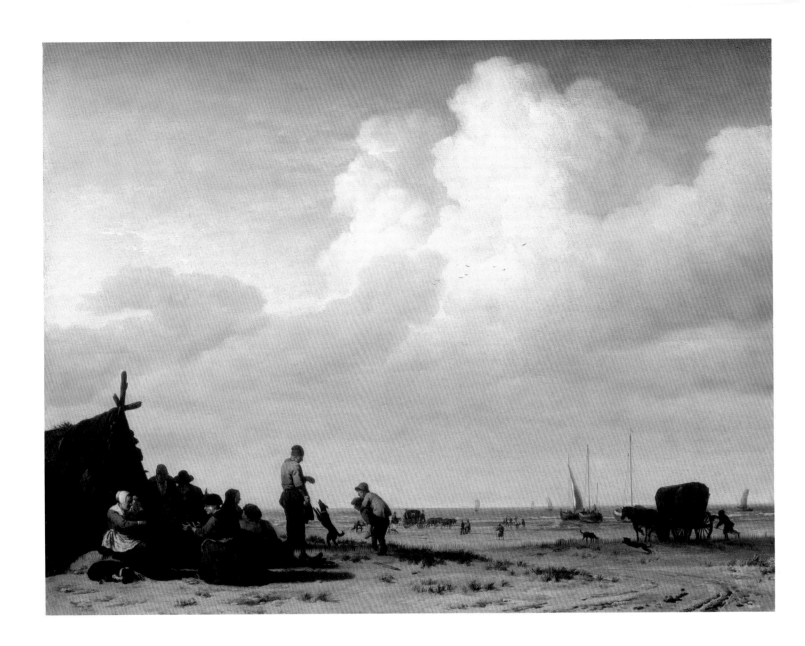

Meindert Hobbema, *The Watermill at Singraven near Denekamp*, 1665–1670
panel, 60 x 84.5 cm
The National Gallery, London

Oh fresh brook flowing free!
Your currents spill so merrily
in crystal streams directed;
How sweet and with such ease
The tumult of the trees
is in your waters reflected!

Jan Harmensz Krul

Jan Harmensz Krul
(1601/2–1646), from:
'Zomer' (*Amstelsche linde*,
1627).

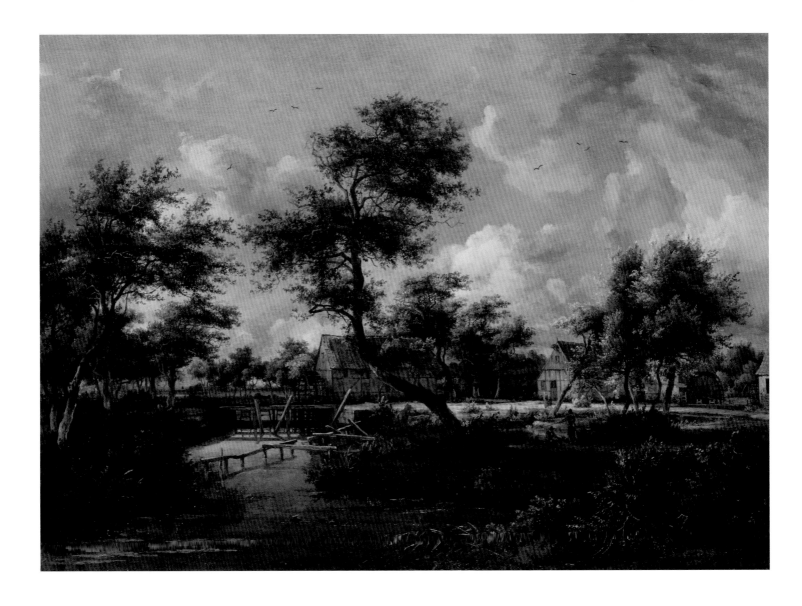

Matthias Withoos, *View of Amersfoort*, 1671
canvas, 249 x 428 cm
Museum Flehite, Amersfoort

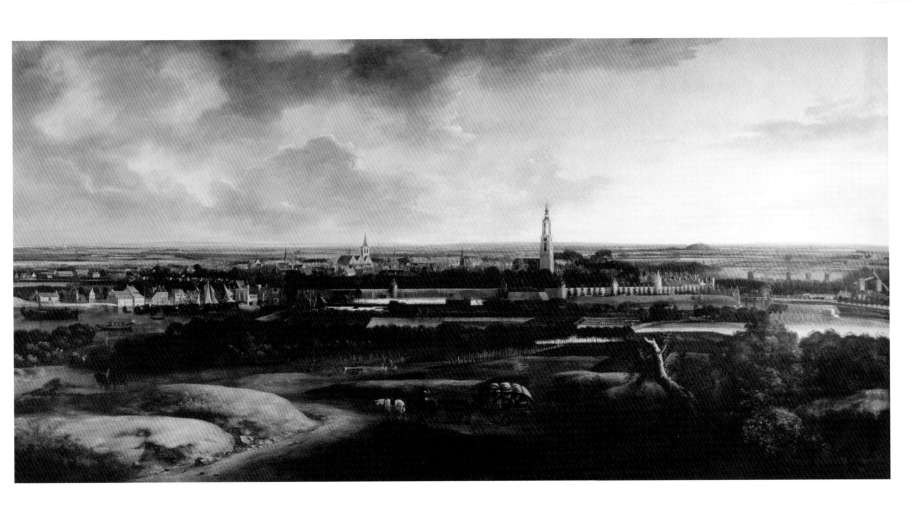

Hendrick ten Oever, *View of Zwolle*, 1675
panel, 87 x 66.7 cm
Torrie Collection, University of Edinburgh, Talbot Rice Gallery of Art, Edinburgh

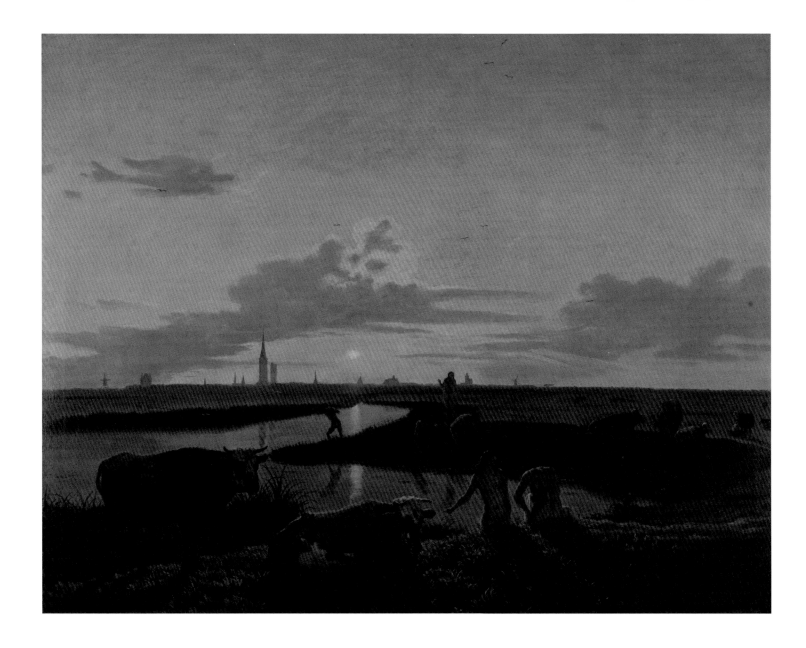

Paulus Constantijn La Fargue, *View of the Bocht van Guinea towards the Wagenbrug (present-day Huygenspark) in The Hague*, 1772
canvas, 38 x 53 cm
Haags Historisch Museum, The Hague

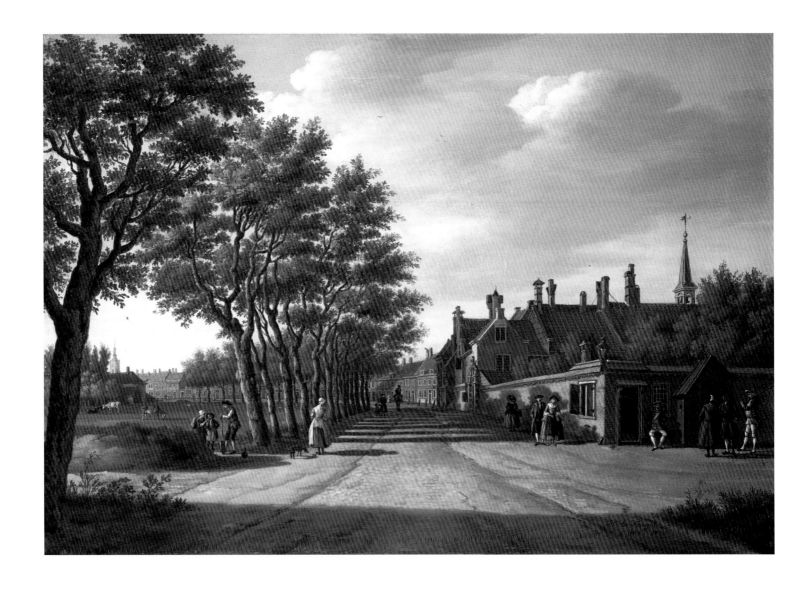

Paulus Constantijn La Fargue, *Rijswijkseweg, The Hague*, 1772
canvas, 38 x 53 cm
Musée des Augustins, Toulouse

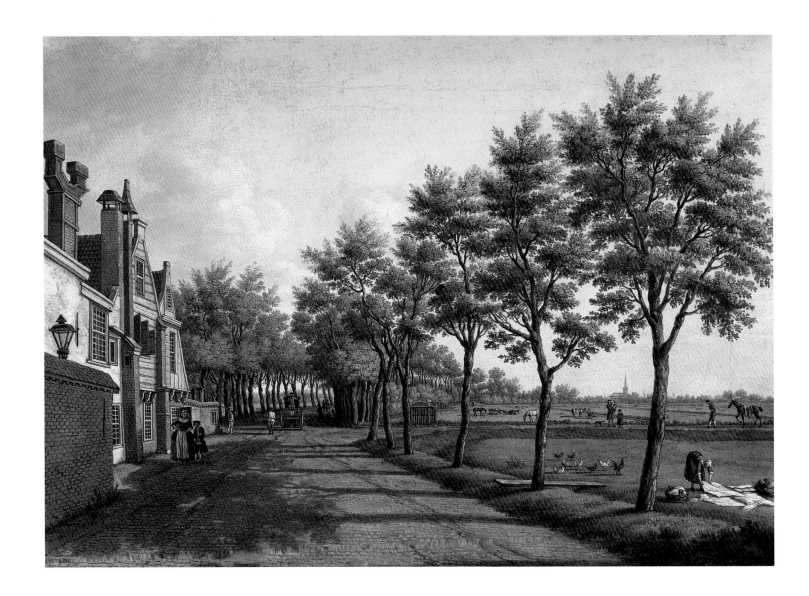

Joris Herst, *Rope-Walk 'de kleingarenbaan' in Gouda*, 1795
canvas, 75 x 57 cm
MuseumgoudA, Gouda

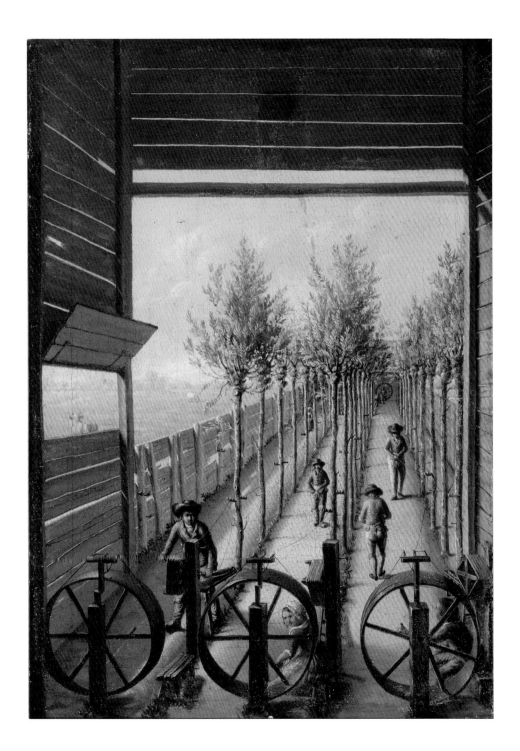

Jan Kamphuijsen, *The Hartelust Estate with a Lady and Gentleman in the Foreground*, 1795
canvas, 55 x 68 cm
Museum van Loon, Amsterdam
On loan from the Amsterdam Historical Museum, Amsterdam

Luxuriant acres, foliage green,
Luscious meadows, frisking herds,
Fresh churned butter, honeyed mead,
Translucent springs, cooling streams,
Refreshing breezes: plenty so rife
lends sweetness to our country life.

Hubert Korneliszoon Poot

Hubert Korneliszoon
Poot (1689–1733), from:
'Akkerleven' (*Gedichten I*,
1716)

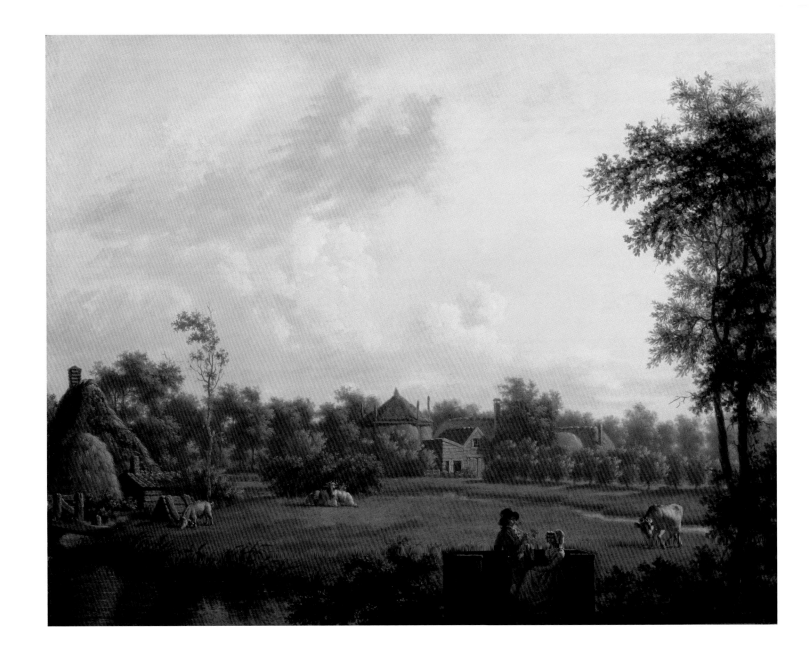

Jan Kamphuijsen, *The Hartelust Estate on the Sloterweg near Amsterdam*, 1795
canvas, 54 x 69 cm
Museum van Loon, Amsterdam
On loan from the Amsterdam Historical Museum, Amsterdam

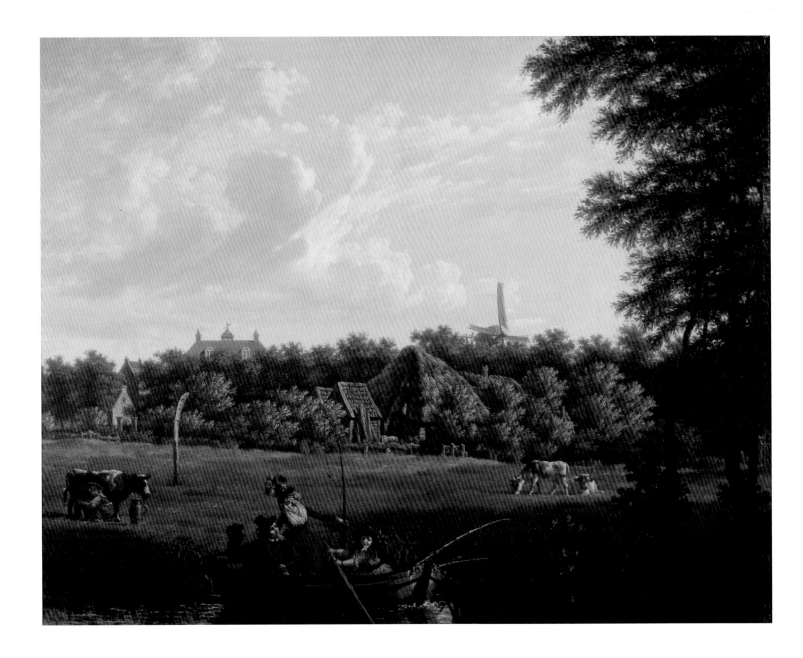

Wouter Johannes van Troostwijk, *Bleaching Field beside a Brook in Gelderland*, 1805–1810
canvas, 53 x 63 cm
Rijksmuseum Twenthe, Enschede
On loan from the Rijksmuseum, Amsterdam

Charming brook that winds its way,
Softly murmuring as it flows
Past its pleasant shady places,
Darkened by the foliage that grows!
Under the oak tree I sit down
On a mossy bed beside your stream.
No care can ever haunt me here
In this heavenly woodland scene.

Elisabeth Maria Post

Elisabeth Maria Post
(1755–1812), from:
'Aan een beek'
(*Gezangen der liefde*, 1794).

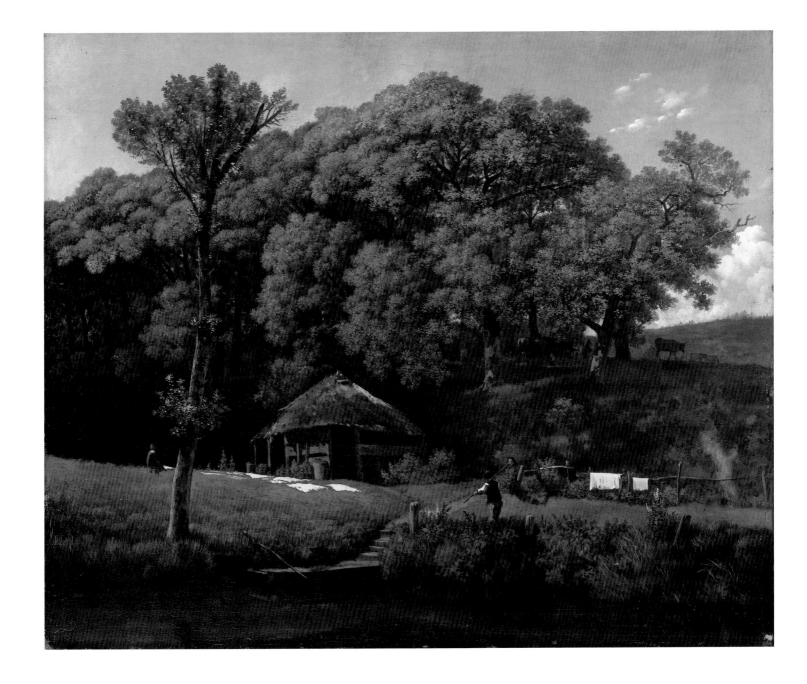

Jacob van Strij, *River Landscape with Trees near Dordrecht*, 1810
canvas, 71 x 95 cm
Dordrechts Museum, Dordrecht

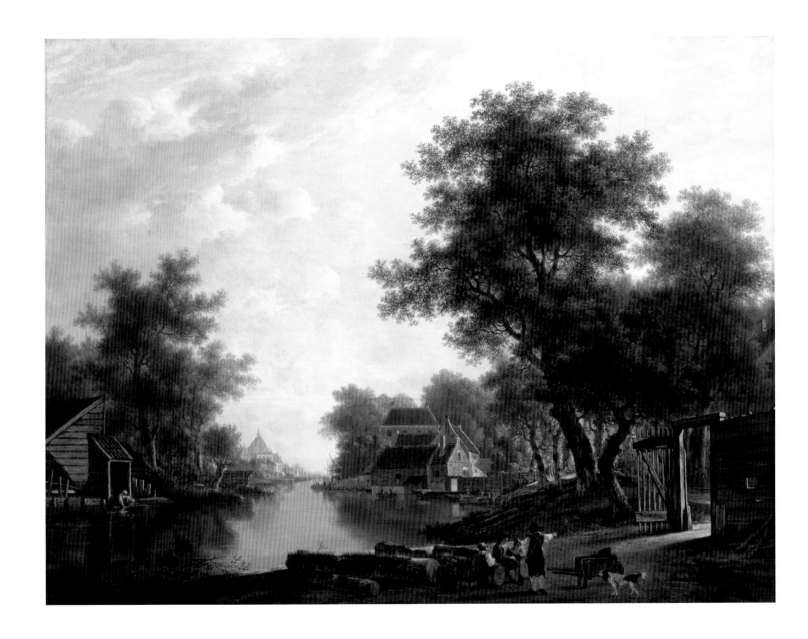

Egbert van Drielst, *View at Eext*, 1810
canvas, 110 x 145 cm
Drents Museum, Assen

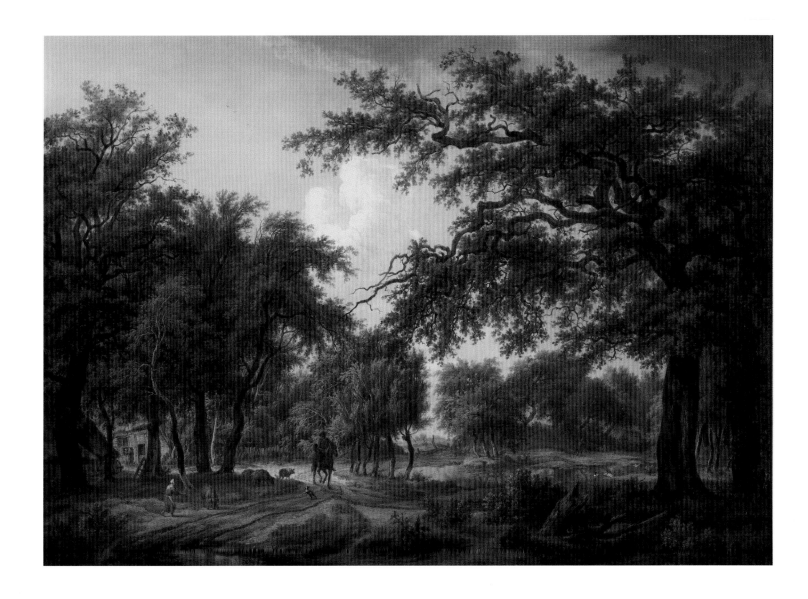

Andreas Schelfhout, *A Farmyard*, 1825–1830
oil on paper on panel, 29 x 28 cm
Rijksmuseum, Amsterdam

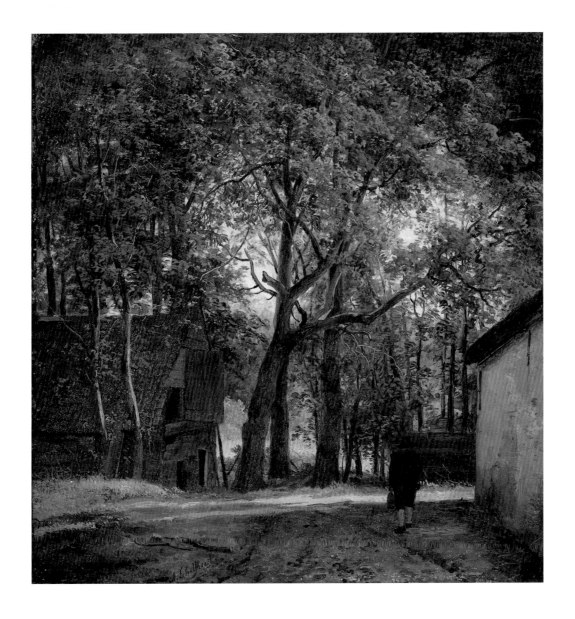

Charles Rochussen, *Racecourse at Scheveningen during the Inauguration on August 3, 1846*, 1846
panel, 32 x 42 cm
Rijksmuseum, Amsterdam

Jan Hendrik Weissenbruch, *View of the Lek near Elshout*, 1850
canvas, 63.5 x 84.5 cm
Teylers Museum, Haarlem

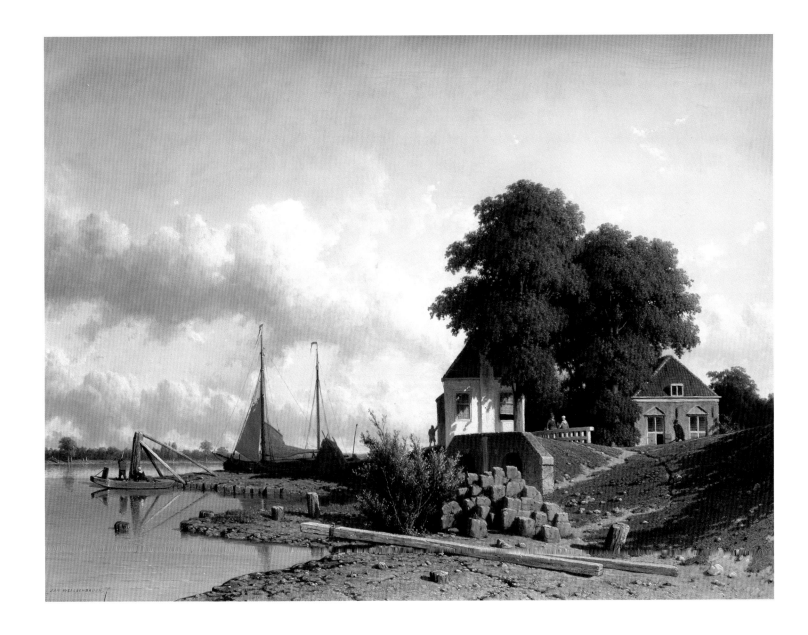

Matthijs Maris, *The Origin (Forest View near Oosterbeek)*, 1860
canvas, 31.5 x 46.4 cm
Gemeentemuseum Den Haag, The Hague

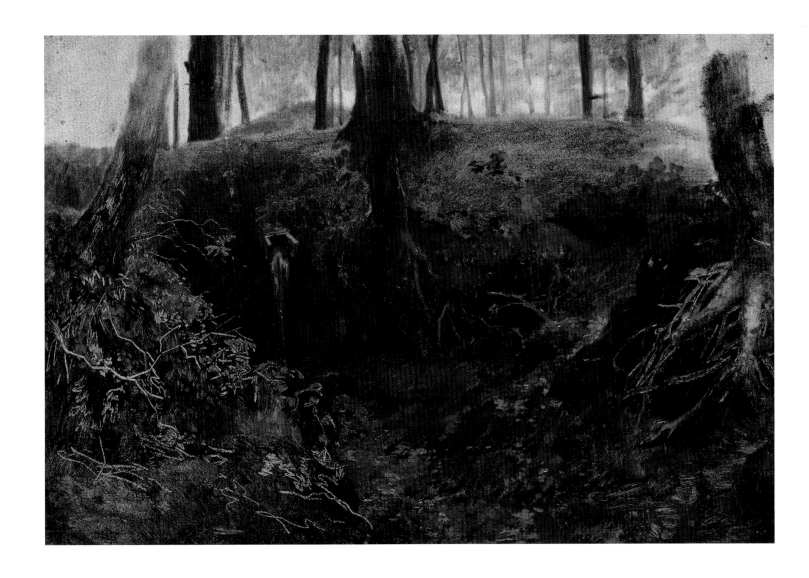

Johan Conrad Greive, *Bombproof Rampart at Vlissingen*, 1860
panel, 33 x 52 cm
Rijksmuseum Amsterdam
On loan from the Amsterdam Historical Museum, Amsterdam

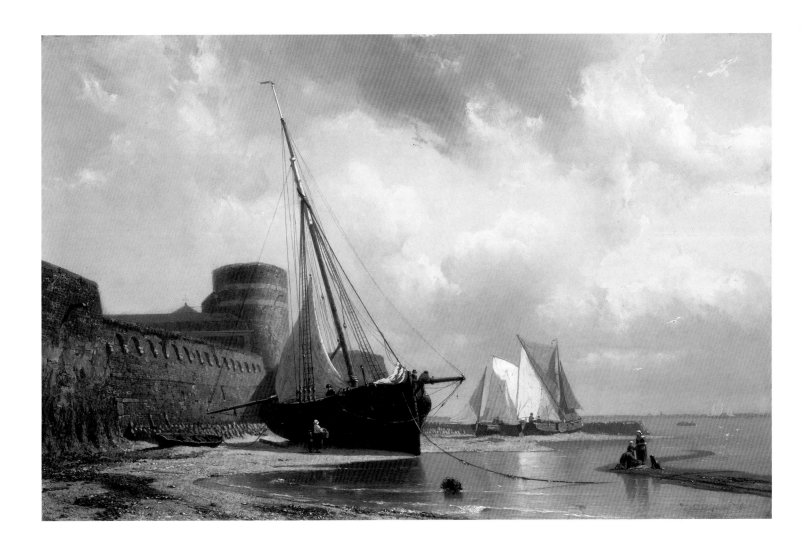

Jacob Maris, *Vegetable Gardens near The Hague*, 1878
canvas, 64 x 55 cm
Gemeentemuseum Den Haag, The Hague

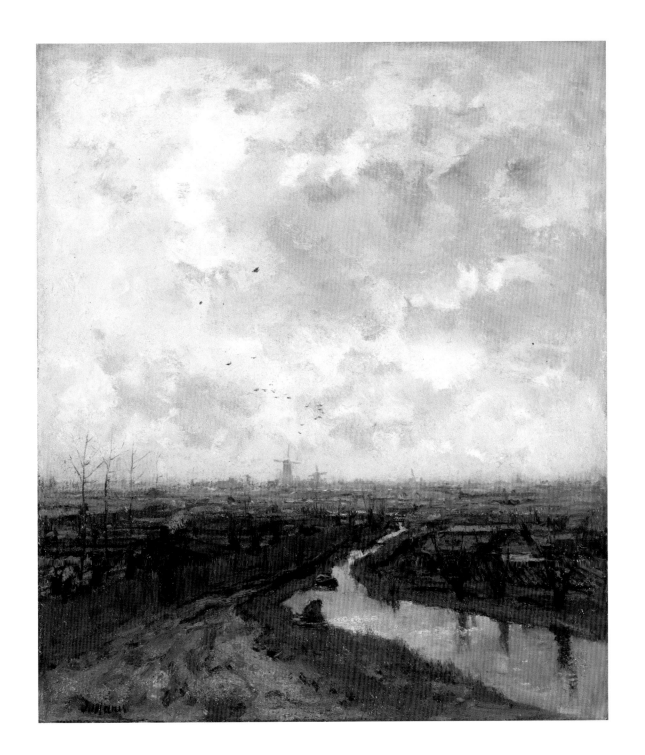

91

Anton Mauve, *A Dutch Road*, 1880
canvas, 50.5 x 36.8 cm
The Toledo Museum of Art, Toledo (Ohio)
Gift of Arthur J. Secor

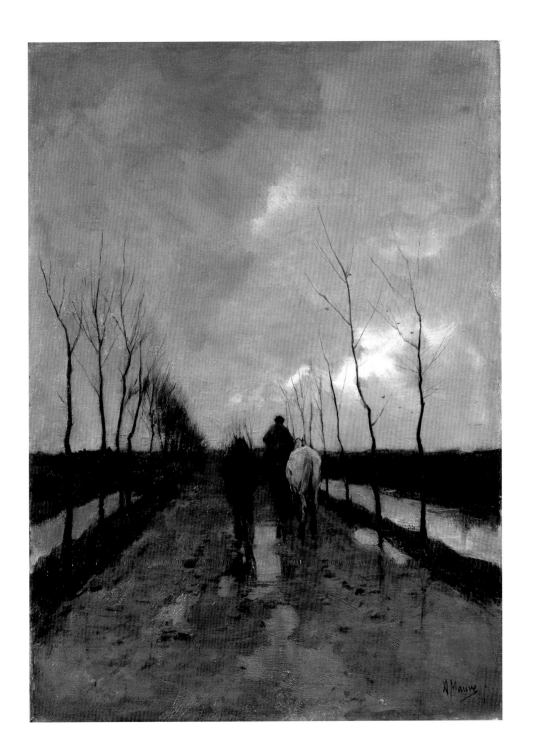

Willem Bastiaan Tholen, *Mills at Giethoorn*, 1882–1884
canvas, 94.5 x 150.5 cm
Private collection

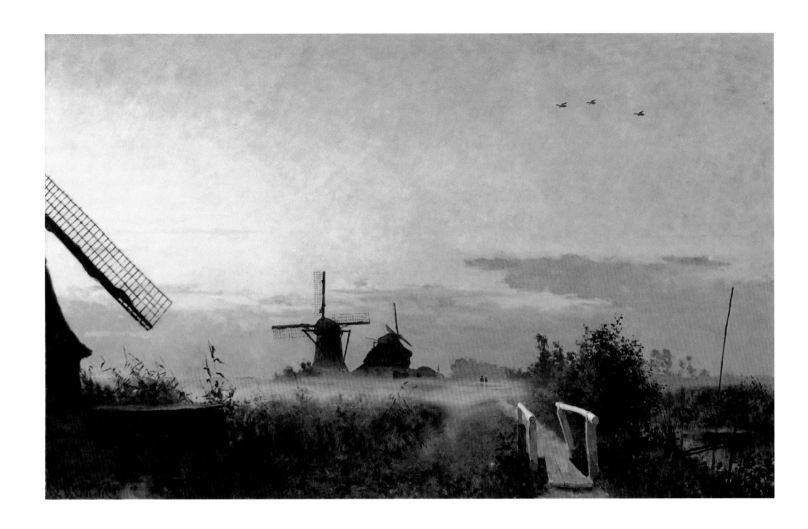

Paul Gabriël, *Watermill near the Leidschedam*, 1884
canvas, 66.6 x 100 cm
Dordrechts Museum, Dordrecht

The windmill standing high on the dam
turns slowly, stiffly spreads its arms.
revolving idly and more idly till
the sails no longer turn at all.
It stands by the pool quite motionless,
As though overcome by drowsiness;
A little sunset red on high
glows in the dark of its window's eye.

Gijsbertus Wilhelmus Lovendaal

Gijsbertus Wilhelmus
Lovendaal (1847–1926),
from: 'Avondliedje'
(*Licht geluid*, 1911).

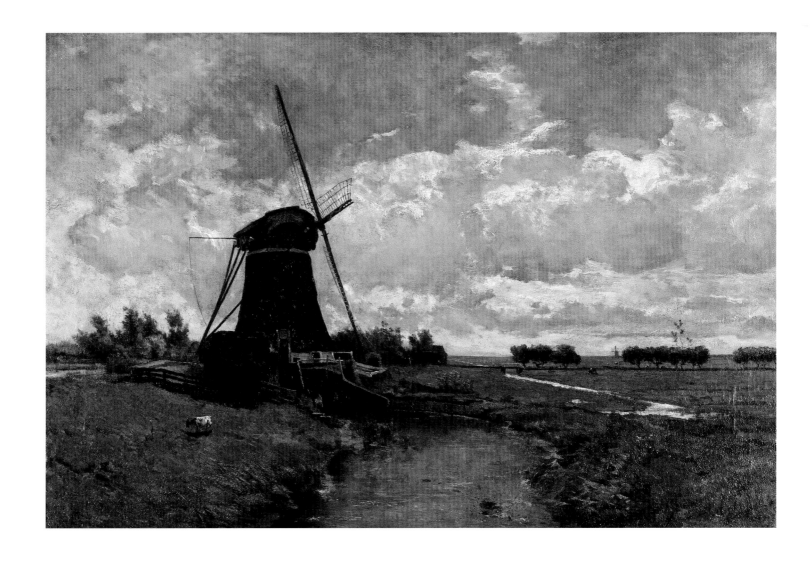

Jan Toorop, *November Afternoon (Willows)*, 1886
canvas, 64.5 x 76.5 cm
Gemeentemuseum Den Haag, The Hague

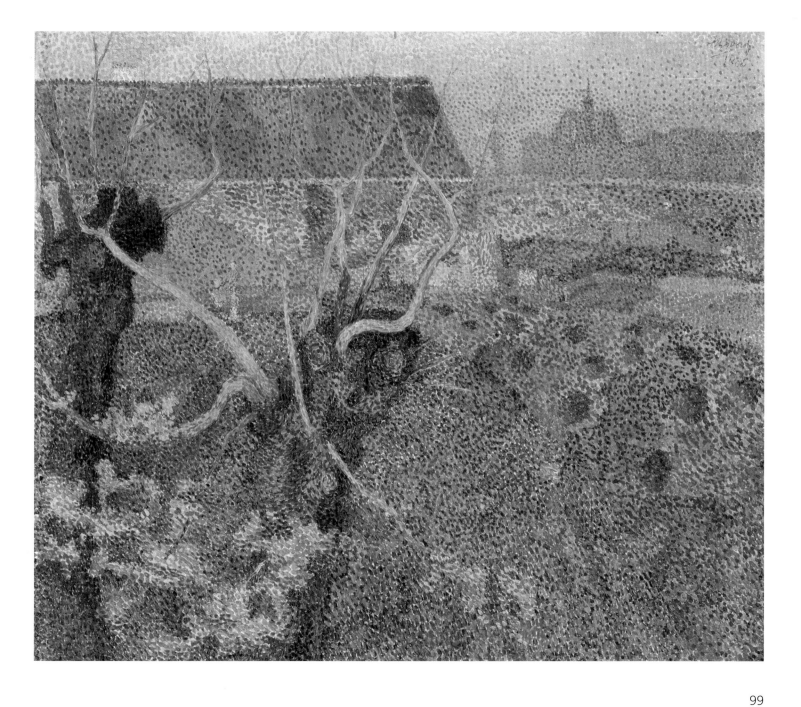

Jan Hendrik Weissenbruch, *Beach View*, 1887
canvas, 64 x 85 cm
Gemeentemuseum Den Haag, The Hague

Grey are your skies, storm-swept your beaches,
Barren your dunes and level your fields,
You made this countryside with a stepmother's hand, –
And yet I love you dearly, oh, my Land!

Everhardus Johannes Potgieter

Everhardus Johannes
Potgieter (1808–1875),
from: 'Holland' (*In Zweden*,
1832)

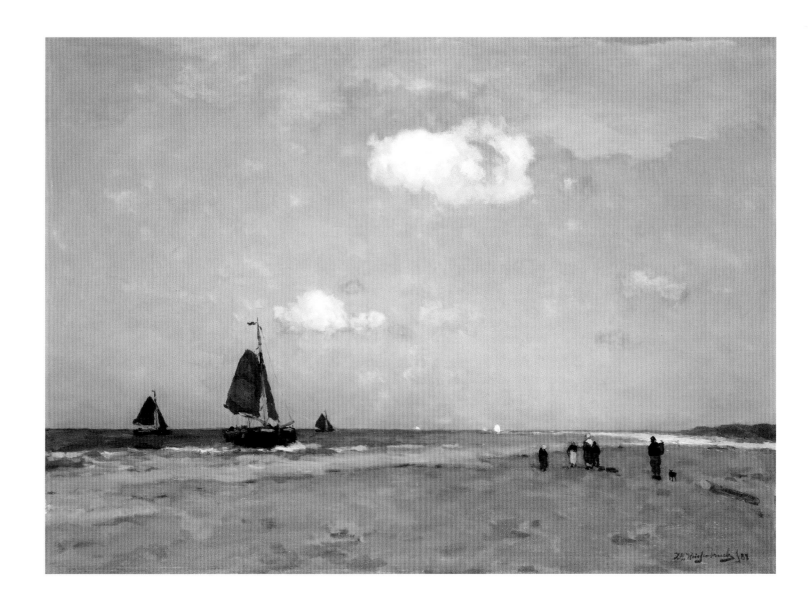

Jan Toorop, *Sea at Katwijk*, 1887
canvas, 86 x 96 cm
Rijksmuseum Amsterdam

The Sea, the Sea breaks with its endless swell,
The Sea that is the mirror of my Soul;
The Sea is like my Soul in essence as in form,
A living Beauty that doesn't know itself.

Willem Theodoor Kloos

Willem Theodoor Kloos
(1859–1938), from
'Van de Zee' (*Verzen*, 1894).

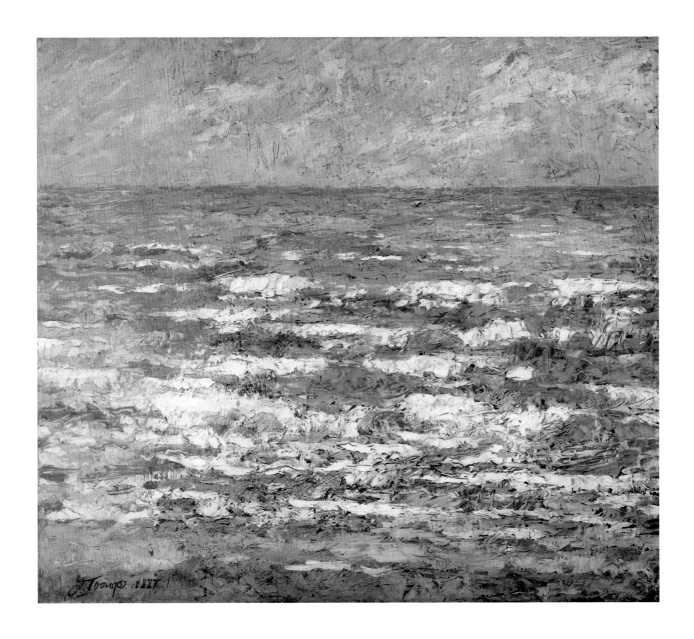

Floris Verster, *Snowy Landscape*, 1895
canvas, 30 x 51 cm
Kröller-Müller Museum, Otterlo

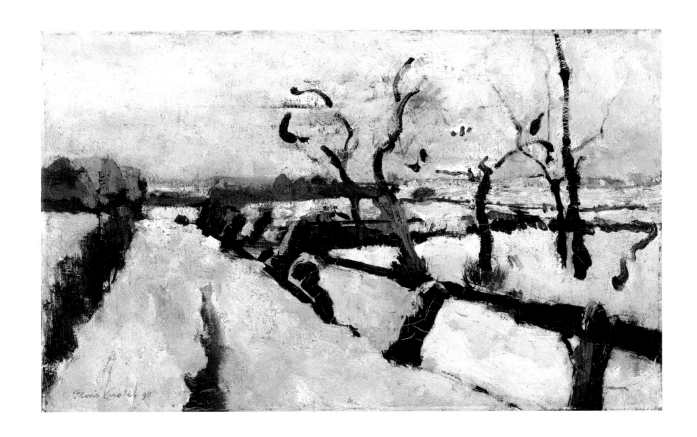

Jan Voerman (the Elder), *Moving Sky*, 1900–1910
panel, 47 x 57 cm
Stedelijk Museum, Kampen

Spring has reached the IJssel near Veecaten.
Clouds and sunlight combine
to make a work by Voerman: an opalescent wrack,
the epitome of Holland, quite sublime.

Ida Gerhardt

Ida Gerhardt (1905–1997),
from: 'Herkenning'
(*Verzamelde gedichten*,
Amsterdam: Athenaeum-
Polak & Van Gennep, 1995)

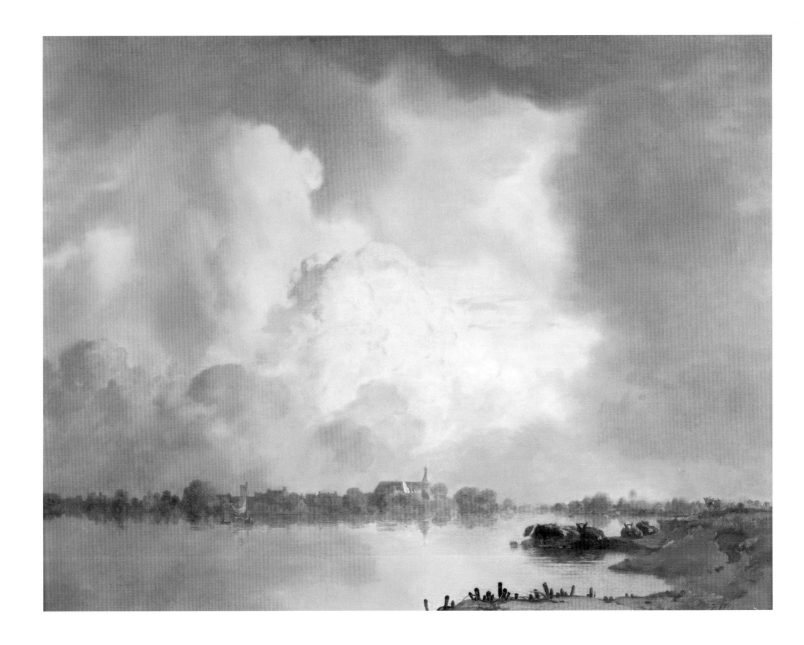

Jan Weissenbruch, *At Noorden near Nieuwkoop*, 1901
canvas, 34 x 41 cm
Dordrechts Museum, Dordrecht
On loan from Instituut Collectie Nederland, Rijswijk/Amsterdam

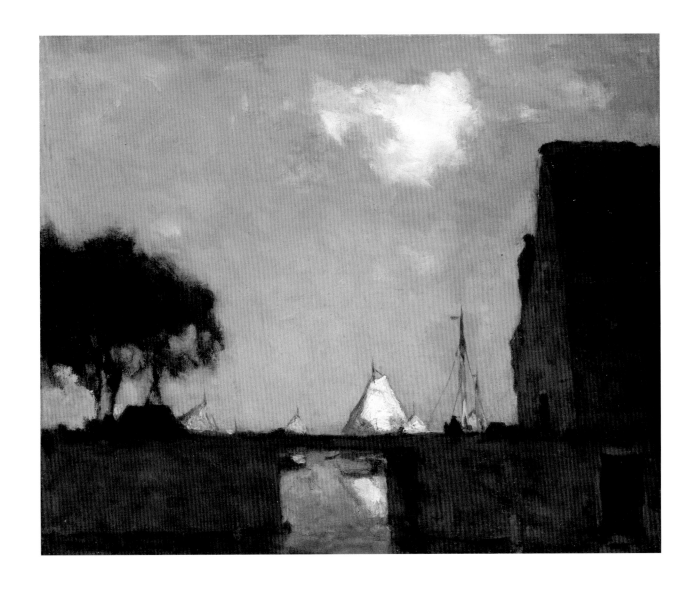

Jan Toorop, *The Veere Fishing Fleet*, 1907
panel, 48 x 62 cm
Centraal Museum, Utrecht

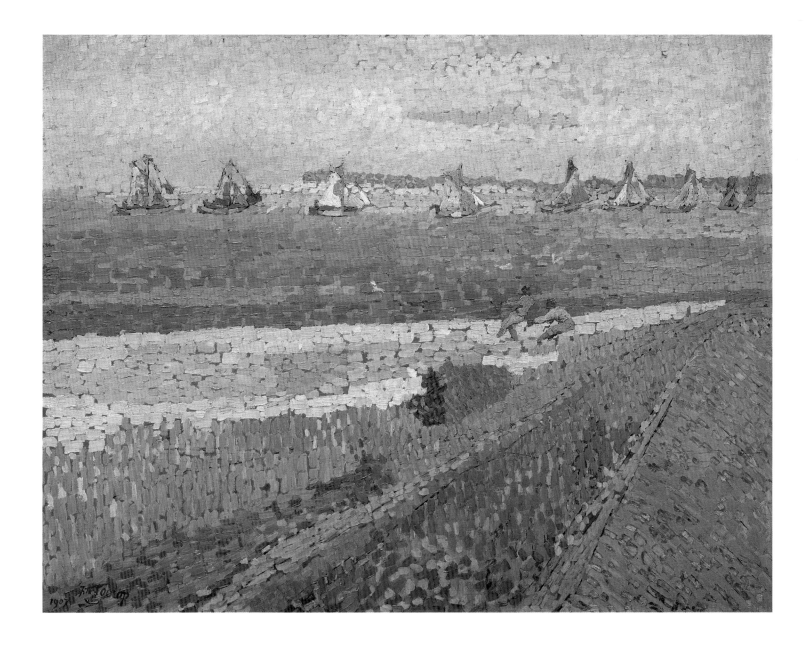

Jan Sluijters, *Moonlit Night IV*, 1912
canvas, 80 x 126 cm
Caldic Collection, Rotterdam

The moon is breaking up the mass of clouds
and streaming from that well eddies and creeks,
glaciers and lakes all break their way
to distant horizons everywhere.

Hendrik Marsman

Hendrik Marsman
(1899–1940), from:
'Maannacht' (*Verzameld
werk*, Amsterdam: Em
Querido's Uitgeverij, 1987).

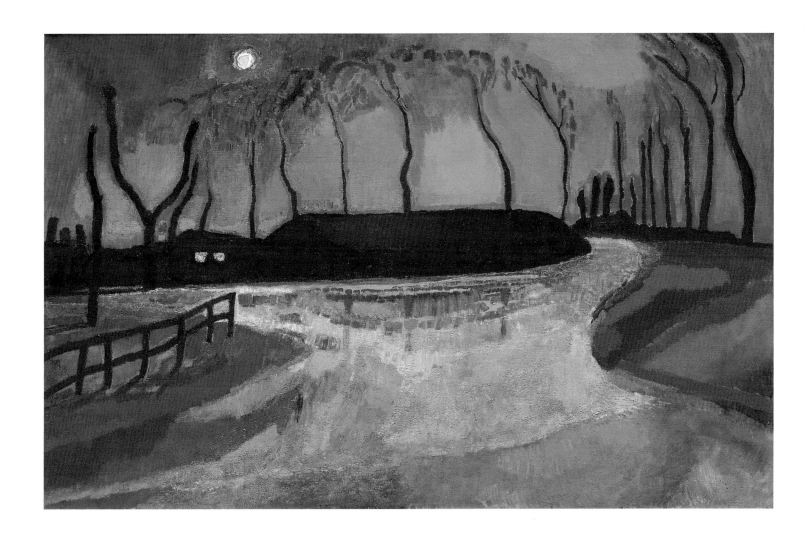

Jan Altink, *The Red Farm*, 1924
canvas, 60.5 x 70.5 cm
Groninger Museum, Groningen

You have knitted your skies over my head:
A heaven rich in sunlight, that the wind makes wild –
I stride rejoicing through these spaces wide,
Or lie against your breast, a suckling child.

Martinus Nijhoff

Martinus Nijhoff
(1894–1953), from:
'Holland' (*Verzamelde
gedichten*, Amsterdam:
Bert Bakker, 2001).

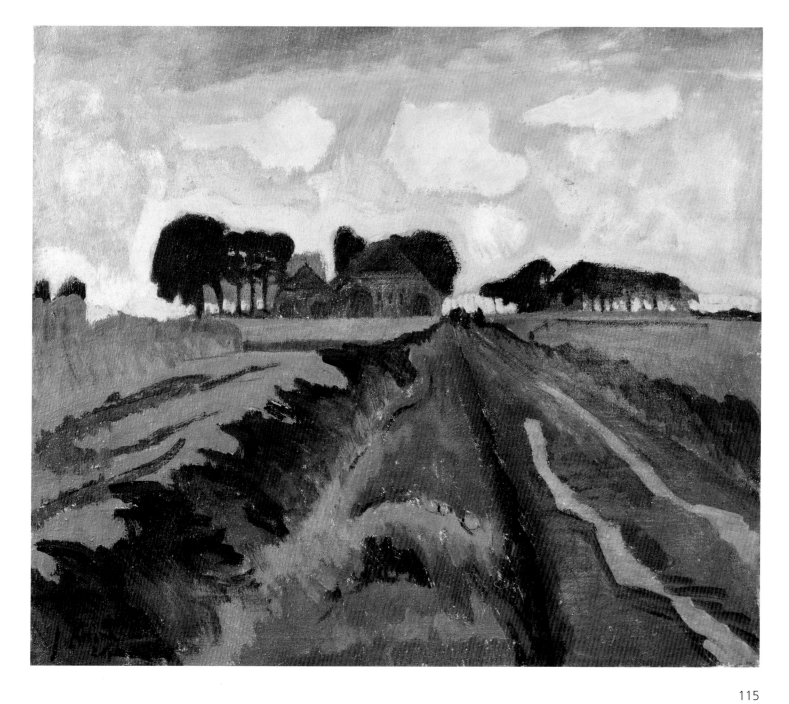

Jan Altink, *Red Cows*, 1927
canvas, 50.5 x 60 cm
Groninger Museum, Groningen
On loan from Stichting de Ploeg, Groningen

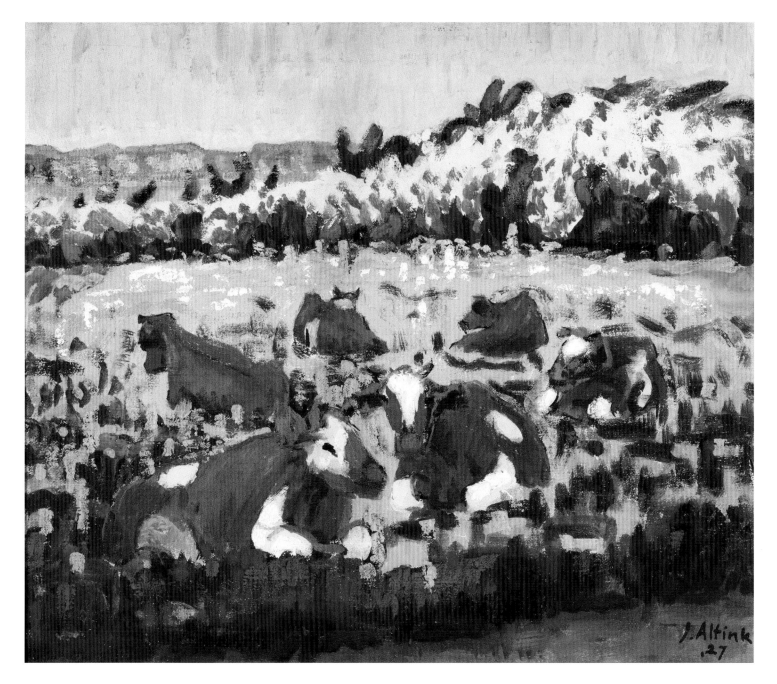

Henk Chabot, *Inundation*, 1944
canvas, 114 x 139 cm
Chabot Museum, Rotterdam

In the wild waters the gentle animals drifted round,
with corn and grass choked in the salty ground,
the highest branches whirled past green locks of hair,
that chattering birds deserted in despair.

M. Vasalis

M. Vasalis (1909–1998),
from: '*Eerst was het
water…*' (Rhyming print,
1946, commemorating
the breaching of the
Wieringermeerdijk during
the last months of the war).

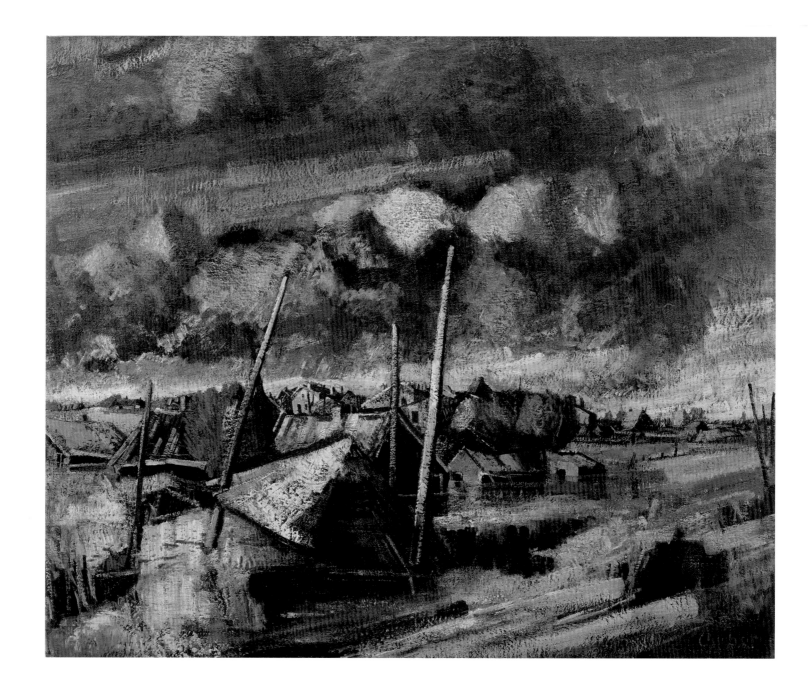

Further publications on the topic of landscape art by the authors

Henk van Os

Het eigene en het andere. Een uitje in de geschilderde natuur (oration University of Amsterdam, 25 April 1997), Amsterdam: Amsterdam University Press, 1997.

'De Ploeg in Bergen – de keuze van Henk van Os, uit drie particuliere collecties', *Kranenburgh Cahier* no. 7, 1999.

'Mancadan. Italianate painter in the remote North', in: A.W.A. Boschloo, E. Grasman and G.J. van der Sman (eds.), *'Aux Quatre Vents'. Festschrift for Bert W. Meijer*, Florence 2002, p. 329-330.

'Russian landscapes: A première', in: D. Jackson and P. Wageman (eds.), *Russian Landscape in the Age of Tolstoy*, exhib.cat. Groningen (Groninger Museum) and London (National Gallery), Schoten (Belgium): BAI, 2004, p. 12-49.

Moederlandse geschiedenis, Essay, CPNB, Amsterdam 2005.

'The painter he findes at his Easill at worke', in: M. van den Doel et al. (eds.), *The Learned Eye. Regarding Art, Theory, and the Artist's Reputation. Essays for Ernst van de Wetering*, Amsterdam: Amsterdam University Press, 2005, p. 206-213.

Dreaming of Italy, exhib.cat. The Hague (Mauritshuis), Zwolle: Waanders, 2006.

'Culturele landverraders', *De Groene Amsterdammer*, 131 (2007) no. 7, p. 28-29; also published as: 'The Italianates: traitors to their Fatherland?', *Kunstchronik*, Heft 7, July 2007, p. 265-267 (on the occasion of the exhibition 'Nicolaes Berchem. In het licht van Italië', Haarlem: Frans Hals Museum, 16 December 2006–15 April 2007).

Huigen Leeflang

— and B. Bakker, *Nederland naar 't leven. Landschapsprenten uit de Gouden Eeuw*, exhib.cat. Amsterdam (Het Rembrandthuis Museum), Zwolle: Waanders 1993.

'Het aards paradijs. Het Haarlemse landschap in 16de- en 17de-eeuwse literatuur en beeldende kunst', in: *De trots van Haarlem. Promotie van een stad in kunst en historie*, exhib.cat. Haarlem (Frans Hals Museum; Teylers Museum), Haarlem 1995, p. 115-126.

'Dutch Landscape: the urban view. Haarlem and its environs in literature and art, 15th–17th-century', in: R. Falkenburg et al. (eds.), *Natuur en landschap in de Nederlandse kunst 1500–1850/Nature and Landscape in Netherlandish Art 1500–1850* (Nederlands Kunsthistorisch Jaarboek 48), Zwolle: Waanders 1998, p. 52-115.

'*Ut Pictura non Poesis* (Painting is not like poetry). Landscape as a subject in 17th century Dutch art', in: *Dutch Art in the Age of Rembrandt and Vermeer. Masterworks of the Golden Age from the Rijksmuseum Amsterdam*, tent.cat. Tokyo (National Museum of Western Art); Aichi (Aichi Prefectural Museum of Art), Tokyo: The Tokyo Shimbun, 2000, p. 39-48, 241-247.

'De natuur van Jacob van Ruisdael', M. Sitt and P. Biesboer (eds.), *Jacob van Ruisdael. De revolutie van het Hollandse landschap*, exhib. cat. Haarlem (Frans Hals Museum), Zwolle: Waanders, 2002, p. 21-27.

Jenny Reynaerts

'*Het karakter onzer Hollandsche school'. De Koninklijke Akademie van Beeldende Kunsten te Amsterdam, 1817–1870*, Leiden: Primavera Pers, 2001.

'"Pour rompre sa routine et varier son talent". Landschapstudies in olieverf van Gilles Closson', in: S. de Bodt, J. Reynaerts and J. de Vries (eds.), *Studiecollectie. Interpretaties van kunst uit de negentiende en twintigste eeuw*, Amsterdam: Vossiuspers, 2001, p. 17-30.

'Momenten uit de 19de-eeuwse schilderspraktijk', *Dordrechts Bulletin*, special issue *Rijksmuseum aan de Merwede, de 19de eeuw op zijn mooist*, 2004, no. 2, p. 17-21.

'De hand van God. Romantiek in de Nederlandse landschapschilderkunst', in: R. de Leeuw, J. Reynaerts and B. Tempel (eds.), *Meesters van de Romantiek. Nederlandse kunstenaars 1800–1850*, Zwolle: Waanders, 2005, p. 95-128.

— and Marguerite Tuyn, 'Naturalisme als uitgangspunt. Piet Mondriaan, *Oostzijdse molen bij maanlicht*', *Bulletin van het Rijksmuseum*, 54 (2006), no. 3, p. 235-246.

About the authors

Henk van Os

Henk van Os studied history and art history at the University of Groningen from 1957–1964 and was admitted to the degree of doctor of Art History (cum laude) in 1969 on the basis of his thesis on 'Iconological Problems in Sienese Painting between 1300 and 1450'. In 1974 he was appointed professor of Art and Cultural History at Groningen University and in 1984 was promoted to dean of the Faculty of Letters. From 1989 to 1996 Van Os was general manager of the Rijksmuseum in Amsterdam. In 1996 he was appointed professor in Art and Society at the University of Amsterdam. Van Os regularly gives guest lectures at foreign universities, including Smith College Northampton (MA), Zentralinstitut für Kunstgeschichte in Munich and Harvard Centre for Renaissance Studies in Florence.

Van Os has become well-known in the Netherlands for his presentations of television programmes on art, namely *Museumschatten* and *Beeldenstorm*.

Louise Fresco

Louise O. Fresco was appointed University Professor of the University of Amsterdam (UvA) in June 2006, and holds a chair in the field of the foundations of sustainable development in an international perspective. Fresco obtained a PhD in tropical crop science cum laude at Wageningen University (NL) in 1986. She also holds visiting professorships at the Institute of Earth Sciences at Stanford University and the David and Lucille Packard Foundation in Palo Alto (US). In addition, she is Distinguished Professor at Wageningen University where she served as Professor of Plant Production Systems from 1990 to 1997. She held the honorary Cleveringa Chair at Leiden University (NL) in 2005–2006. Fresco served as Assistant Director-General of the Agriculture Department of the FAO (the UN Food and Agriculture Organization in Rome) until 2006. Fresco has published extensively in both scientific journals and in the popular media. She writes a syndicated column and participates in many national and international radio and television programmes. She has published seven non-scientific books in Dutch (among which three novels).

Huigen Leeflang

Huigen Leeflang has been involved in producing exhibitions and catalogues for several Dutch museums including the Frans Hals Museum in Haarlem, De Lakenhal in Leiden and the Rijksmuseum Amsterdam (*Dawn of the Golden Age*, 1993). His contributions in the landscape sphere include the exhibition 'Nederland naar 't leven. Landschapsprenten uit de Gouden Eeuw' in the Rembrandthuis in 1993. Since 2002 he has been curator of prints in the Print Room of the Rijksmuseum Amsterdam. In 2003–2004, together with the Metropolitan Museum in New York, he mounted the exhibition 'Hendrick Goltzius, Dutch Master (1558–1617): Drawings, Prints, and Paintings'. Huigen Leeflang is attached to the Master Curators in Training (joint-project of the two Amsterdam Universities UvA and VU), the Amsterdam Summer University, and is also on the board of the Werkgroep Zeventiende Eeuw.

Jenny Reynaerts

Jenny Reynaerts is curator of 19th- and 20th-century paintings at the Rijksmuseum Amsterdam. Prior to this she worked as a lecturer in the Art History Department of Amsterdam University. In 2000 she was admitted to the degree of doctor on the basis of her book, '*Het karakter onzer Hollandsche school*'. *De Koninklijke Akademie van Beeldende Kunsten te Amsterdam, 1817–1870*. Reynaerts has assisted in mounting several exhibitions on Dutch art, including 'Schilders van Tachtig. Nederlandse schilderkunst 1880–1895', 'Stemmingen. Willem Witsen (1860–1923)' in 2003, 'De 19de eeuw op zijn mooist. Rijksmuseum aan de Merwede' in 2004, and 'Meesters van de Romantiek. Nederlandse kunstenaars 1800–1850' in 2005. From 2003 to 2006 she was the editor of the Dutch *Jaarboek voor Vrouwengeschiedenis*. She is presently a member of the Advisory Panel on Art for the Prince Bernhard Cultural Fund and is also on the Art Editorial Board of Amsterdam University Press. In 2008 she became a committee member of the Werkgroep Negentiende eeuw.

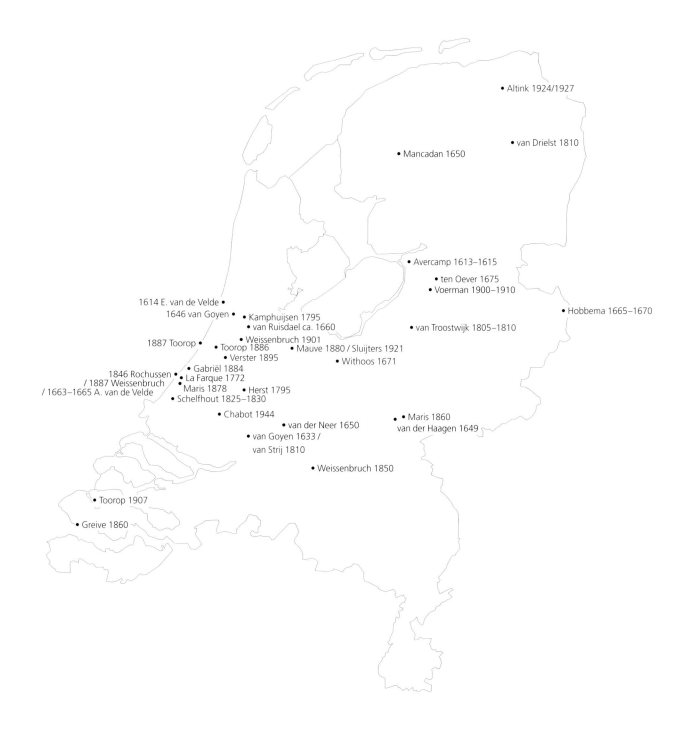

• Altink 1924/1927

• van Drielst 1810

• Mancadan 1650

• Avercamp 1613–1615

• ten Oever 1675
• Voerman 1900–1910

1614 E. van de Velde •
1646 van Goyen •
• Kamphuijsen 1795
• van Ruisdael ca. 1660
• Hobbema 1665–1670

• van Troostwijk 1805–1810

1887 Toorop •
• Weissenbruch 1901
• Toorop 1886   • Mauve 1880 / Sluijters 1921
• Verster 1895
• Withoos 1671

• Gabriël 1884
1846 Rochussen • • La Farque 1772
/ 1887 Weissenbruch   • Maris 1878   • Herst 1795
/ 1663–1665 A. van de Velde
• Schelfhout 1825–1830

• Chabot 1944
• van der Neer 1650   • Maris 1860
van der Haagen 1649
• van Goyen 1633 /
van Strij 1810

• Weissenbruch 1850

• Toorop 1907

• Greive 1860

This book was published on the occasion of the Apeldoorn International Triennial from 11 June till 28 September 2008.

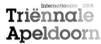

Internationale 2008
Triënnale Apeldoorn

This publication accompanied the exhibition 'The Discovery of the Netherlands' at CODA Museum in Apeldoorn (11 June to 28 September 2008).

The exhibition was made possible by a generous contribution from the Stichting Triënnale Apeldoorn, Prins Bernhard Cultuurfonds, VSBfonds and Rabobank Apeldoorn en Omstreken.

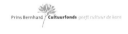

Prins Bernhard / **Cultuurfonds** geeft cultuur de kans

VSBfonds

Exhibition:
Concept: prof.dr. Henk van Os in collaboration with dr. Jenny Reynaerts, drs. Huigen Leeflang and drs. Carin Reinders
Design: Wim Crouwel
Production: CODA Museum, Apeldoorn

Publication:
Foreword: Carin Reinders
Authors: prof.dr. Henk van Os (in collaboration with dr. Jenny Reynaerts, drs. Huigen Leeflang) and prof.dr. ir. Louise Fresco
Selection of poetry quotations:
Klaas van den Hoek, Nieuwe alinea, Amsterdam
Translation: Wendie Shaffer (essay Henk van Os), Kate Williams (Foreword, essay Louise Fresco), Donald Gardner (poetry quotations)
Design: Wim Crouwel
Typesetting: Bregt Balk
Lithography and printing: Drukkerij Die Keure, Bruges
Paper: Satimat 170 grs
Binding: Brepols
Project coordination: Barbera van Kooij, NAi Publishers
Publisher: NAi Publishers, Rotterdam

Photocredits:
The photograph of Amersfoort on p. 26 was taken by Cor van de Braber, with thanks to Bekking & Blitz Publishers.
The reproductions of the paintings in this publication have been put at the disposal of CODA by the lenders.

The organizers would like to thank:
William Loohuis, registrar CODA
Pauline W. Kruseman and Norbert Middelkoop, Amsterdams Historisch Museum
Joop van Caldenborgh, Caldic Collection BV
Pauline Terreehorst, Centraal Museum
Mrs C. Grootveld-Prins and Mrs J.N. Bijlsma, Chabot Museum
Peter Schoon and Sander Paarlberg, Dordrechts Museum
Michel van Maarseveen, Drents Museum
John Scally, Talbot Rice Gallery
Wim van Krimpen, Gemeentemuseum Den Haag
Kees van Twist and Patty Wageman, Groninger Museum
Antoinette Visser, Haags Historisch Museum
Evert van Straaten, Kröller-Müller Museum
Frits J. Duparc, Emilie Gordenker and Peter van der Ploeg, Mauritshuis
Philippe de Montebello, Walter Liedtke and Lisa Cain, Metropolitan Museum of Art
Alain Daguerre de Hureaux, Musée des Augustins
Gerard de Kleijn and Onno Maurer, Museum Flehite
Tonko Grever, Museum van Loon
Ranti Tjan, MuseumgoudA
Martin Wyld, Betsy Wieseman, Marjorie E. Wieseman and Perry Chapman, National Gallery
Ronald de Leeuw and Taco Dibbets, Rijksmuseum Amsterdam
Mrs Dr. D.A.S. Cannegieter, Rijksmuseum Twenthe
René van Mierlo, Stedelijk Museum Kampen
Marjan Scharloo, Teylers Museum
Don Bacigalupi, Lawrence W. Nichols en Patricia Whitesides, Toledo Museum of Art
The Dutch and Belgian owners who courteously loaned paintings from their private collections.

For works of visual artists affiliated with a CISAC-organization the copyrights have been settled with Pictoright in Amsterdam. © 2008, c/o Pictoright Amsterdam

NAi Publishers is an internationally orientated publisher specialized in developing, producing and distributing books on architecture, visual arts and related disciplines.
www.naipublishers.nl info@naipublishers.nl

Available in North, South and Central America through D.A.P./Distributed Art Publishers Inc, 155 Sixth Avenue 2nd Floor, New York, NY 10013-1507, Tel 212 6271999, Fax 212 6279484.

Available in the United Kingdom and Ireland through Art Data, 12 Bell Industrial Estate, 50 Cunnington Street, London W4 5HB, Tel 208 7471061, Fax 208 7422319.

Printed and bound in Belgium

ISBN 978-90-5662-027-1

Cover:
Hendrick ten Oever, *View of Zwolle*, 1675